Overcoming
the
Hand you
were
Dealt

Kisha Taylor

Overcoming the Hand you were Dealt

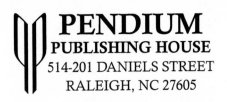

PENDIUM
PUBLISHING HOUSE
514-201 DANIELS STREET
RALEIGH, NC 27605

For information, please visit our Web site at
www.pendiumpublishing.com

PENDIUM Publishing and its logo
are registered trademarks.

Overcoming The Hand You Were Dealt
by Kisha Taylor

Book cover inspired by Deja's mom

ISBN: 978-1-944348-40-3

This book is printed on acid-free paper.

Gratitude

Thank you in advance to all who will read this book. Please share it, for there are many women who struggle and who have been hurt, betrayed and unappreciated, all while being blessed at the same time.

Inspiration

This book was inspired by my dear friend Tyra, who suggested I should write a book during a conversation about my life and an incident I was living through. I kind of shrugged it off, but it resonated, as I had thought about this over the years and others frequently suggested it to me. This was due to my life experiences and my desire, once I retire, to speak to young women about overcoming life's challenges. My goal is to speak to women in places like prisons, halfway houses, colleges, churches, women's groups, etc. I thank Tyra, who I have known since I was 10, for being the straw that broke the camel's back and actually pushed me to finally start writing.

Contents

A Prayer From A Friend

I prayed for God to give me the right words to say. With tears rolling down my face, the Holy Spirit simply said, "Pray." So, Lord I thank you for Deja'. Father, you have given her such a heart. Lord, many people would have been consumed by all that life has given her. But Father, you have given her strength beyond strength. I ask that you continue to cover her by your blood, Lord. Bless her! Continue to guide and govern her every step. Protect her and clear every path that you have anointed her to journey on. Father, she is so dear to me. Keep her in perfect peace. She loves you with all her heart. Lord, I ask that you fill every gap in her life the way only you can. Complete her. You have given me more than a best friend, more than a sister. Deja' is a gift that you blessed the world with. I thank you for her. In Jesus' precious name, Amen!

Introduction

Have you ever experienced a day that you can point to when your life made a pivot? I have had several pivot moments in my life. Some were due to ill-intended people who sought to harm me; some were due to unsupportive or selfish people in my circle; some came from people who loved and challenged me to grow; and others came simply because of much needed self-evaluation.

Recently I had another pivot moment, and like the ones in the past, it once again took me to a new level, and this book was born. This day I am speaking of came after I had several amazing experiences, all of which took place in a period of only a few weeks.

I was in a place of feeling overwhelmed and back on my heels with hands raised, trying to hold up a wall that was bearing down on me. First, I had recently gone through a breakup with a man I had been seeing for a year, only to find out, about a month after the breakup, that he had deceived me from the beginning and was not a man of his word.

Second, when I shared my disappointment about this man with friends, one in particular responded in a way that deeply hurt my feelings. What someone says can damage or encourage you during painful times. She appeared not to have any care for my pain in that moment, although it was not intentional, and she did apologize, as we have for years supported one another on many occasions. Nonetheless I felt she was less than compassionate and minimized my pain as unimportant. It was a missed "be there for your friend" moment.

Third, during this same period of time I was doing work on one of my properties and had not long before purchased a fifth property. I am a planner, therefore I planned out a budget and expenses to do the work on the fourth property based on my contractor's findings months earlier. I did the calculations and was confident about closing the deal on the fifth property without issue or financial burden. I was therefore dismayed to receive a call from the tenant, only two months after she moved in, informing me that the front door would not close. Apparently the contractor missed this problem during the evaluation. Needless to say, $20,000 later, I had to repair the foundation. This absorbed almost all of my savings and caught me way off guard. I knew that if something else unexpected occurred before having the chance to regroup, I would be in a situation.

I asked a family member if I could tap her on the shoulder if I needed some help. I stated it might not be needed, but wanted to plan ahead just in case. I wanted a resource I could count on who had the means. I don't want to appear unappreciative because she has helped with short-term projects in the past and I have always reimbursed her when I said I would. Thankfully I did not need the help, because nothing major happened and therefore I had room to recover.

People who know me know I do not ask for help unless it is absolutely needed! I am usually the person offering help, not asking for it. I try my best not to be a burden but instead to be a burden lifter for others as often as I can. This is sometimes a double-edged sword, because people view me as being able to handle any- and everything, and therefore unbreakable, never vulnerable, or in need of sensitivity and support.

When you have a dream it does require discipline, strength and action; without them there are no rewards. Yet in no way does that make me invincible. Sometimes you have to scratch, crawl, sacrifice and fight to bring your dream to pass. At times you even have to ask for help.

I am unapologetic about my ability to focus and chase my dreams despite the odds, and neither should you be! Just know that even the strongest of people experience times of weakness and need others they can count on during their vulnerable moments also.

Nonetheless, the response of my family member floored me, as she is someone very close to me, someone I would do and have done just about anything for over the course of my life. She never got back to me regarding the request for possible help. I would understand if she came back and said, No, I'm not in a position to help, and offered some encouragement at minimum. Instead she acted as if I never asked for help and avoided talking about it. I brought it up again about a week or so later and she said, "What if something else goes wrong? Maybe you should not have purchased the fifth house, and why don't you just ask your ex-husband?"

I was now beyond hurt, not because I could not ask him, and he would most certainly have helped, but because first, she avoided me, then suggested asking my ex-husband, and she was blood! The hurtful part was that if anything ever happened to her, I would sell everything I had to help her at a moment's notice without hesitation. Therefore the thought of knowing she had the means to help me, yet if in a bad situation, she would hesitate? Really!

It made me feel she did not believe in me and was not willing to make the same sacrifice that would be made for her, and it hurt me to the core. I shared my feelings with her and she apologized, saying she was nervous but should have expressed her concerns instead of avoiding the matter.

Fourth, as if the first three blows were not plenty, yes, there is still more. While I was managing each of those blows I was also having challenges at work. There were constant demands and changes that needed to be made to meet the requests of the powers that be that I "do more with less." There were new agendas needing to be rolled out to ensure success, and it all needed to happen swiftly and with precision. However, not everyone on the team was fully on board and understanding of the vision and the purpose. Therefore there was a battle of wills taking place in the office.

The final thing was really mostly shocking and disappointing. I attended my godson's wedding and my ex-husband showed up with a woman who he had some form of involvement with many years ago, while he and I were together. He did not remember until she introduced herself and I recognized her name, which was a rather unique and memorable name. I gave him a look that said, "You can't be serious right now!" At that moment, he realized I remembered this woman from the past and the look on his face was one of embarrassment.

I felt blindsided. As close as we are, why didn't he just tell me, I thought. I would not have been angry; we both have dated and respected one another over the years since our divorce. I would have simply been prepared for it. Instead I was left in shock, feeling deceived and wondering if this woman knew who I was, yet was boldly standing in my face smiling and shaking my hand.

With all of this brewing inside all at once, over several weeks, the day of reckoning came. Everything came to a breakthrough. It was a Saturday morning in December. I had an ordained appointment with a pivot!

It was a pivot that ushered me out of my old path and into a new season in life that I was not expecting. I experienced a deeper realization of knowing that some people are really selfish, regardless of the depth of the relationship. They are willing to receive your love, support, assistance and sacrifices made for them, claiming verbally to appreciate you, yet falling short when it comes to returning love and support when you need it.

A new perspective and mission was born that Saturday morning regarding people in my life in general. A discerning of sorts for those I should compartmentalize differently with a greater awareness of how they view me in terms of value and importance in their lives. Some people whom you regard highly amaze you when they fall short when you need them most, emotionally or as a support system or partner. Others love and support you, in spite of yourself, flaws and all.

I have had both kinds of people in my life and they have revealed themselves in different situations. My challenge, however, is that I tend to blur the lines, at times thinking everyone is willing to do for me what I am willing to do for them. They always bring me back to reality in certain situations. I then see clearly in those moments, and it serves as a reminder that most people are selfish by nature.

Some situations are innocent, of course, and are part of relationships with people. Nonetheless, it does not change the feeling you get when they hurt you. I have had many people in my life who have been there for me in really trying times, yet some of those same people have brought hurt and disappointment also. I still cherish those relationships and am grateful for them, because we all are human and have caused hurt to others even unintentionally. However, this sequence of events, all happening at once, caused me to reevaluate *all* of my relationships, past, present and those to come; and I presume it all happened for a reason.

I was like, God, what is this all about? I wasn't depressed, crying or even angry. I was just like, f... it and everyone too.

I made a comment to my mom, who responded, "Wow, that said a lot." What I said was, I am all things to all people, but I am nothing to anyone. She was shocked to hear me say that, but that was where I was at that moment, asking God what in the world was going on. A question I found myself asking at other intersections along my journey as well. But I will tell you, it all has been a blessing. Muscles do not form without resistance and a rose does not bloom without sun and watering.

So I thank all the people, throughout my life, who have bruised me, betrayed me, nearly caused me to lose my mind, smiled in my face while consorting with others behind my back, claimed to have my back like a jacket yet left me naked, abandoned me and threw me under the bus to others...SMH!

God is always my keeper though, not man. If you agree, say Amen!

If you can relate to any of what I just shared, then this book is for you. It will either give you freedom, help you go through your process with more peace, give you confirmation or, at minimum, for those who have healed, offer relatability.

As I write this book, there are songs that, if you listen to them, will reveal to you the emotion and the heart behind my words and my experiences, and they can be a part of your encouragement and healing, too.

So please listen to:
Hezekiah Walker, "God Favored Me"
Tamela Mann, "God Provides"
Charles Jenkins, "War"
Marvin Sapp, "Never Would Have Made It"
John P. Kee, "Life & Favor (You Don't Know My Story)"
William Murphy, "It's Working"
Tasha Cobb, "Break Every Chain"
Yolanda Adams, "Open My Heart"
Mary Mary, "Go Get It"
Marvin Winans, "I'm Over It Now"
Gladys Knight "The Need To Be"
Brian Courtney Wilson, "Worth Fighting For"

Chapter One
Broken Beginnings

Life has a funny way of expressing itself. There are many people who have had various experiences that have either weakened them or strengthened them.

Think about Deja', a child born to Mia, a 17-year-old girl who had no identity of her own and was clueless about raising a child. Mia's relationship with her mom was not one of affection, support and closeness, and she did not know who her father was, either. Therefore, how could Mia know how to have a mother-daughter relationship with her new baby?

She left Deja' with her mom, Alma, until she was around two, and then decided she would take on the role of motherhood. That was when the journey began for Deja', who would have to face a world of heartache, pain, struggle, betrayal, abuse, and abandonment in order to get to accomplishments, blessings, peace and joy, all while getting to know herself and God. She led a life of trials and tests to overcome the hand that was dealt to her, and is still overcoming them to this day.

How many of you reading this can go back that far in your life and see where it all started for you? I believe you have to take the time to go back and see where it started for you and the experiences you had that set you on your

course, so you are then able to see what hand you were
dealt and what your process was, is, or should be to get you
to a place of peace and wholeness.

Now that I have your attention, and you have scanned
your memory bank to get a view at your beginnings, let
me give you a view of this young girl who is now 46. I
will show you her journey in the hope that you can see
yourself in her and some of what she overcame, to help
you identify yourself and know you can also. Although she
is still on her journey, you can relate and take away some
things that she did—effectively and not so effectively—that
can encourage you and allow you to give yourself credit for
the things you did better, because if you are in any way like
Deja', you are probably very hard on yourself. If not, then
at minimum know that you are not alone, and with God all
things are possible.

I am making this book simple, transparent and plain
for you, in hopes that you see yourself in Deja' or share it
with someone you know who will be strengthened by this
young girl's journey.

Deja' had no father growing up and Mia, her mom,
was 17. Her biological father was a petty thief who was
killed by a cab driver when she was in Mia's womb. Deja'
was born prematurely due to the stress placed on her
mom. Ironically she was born with three 7s—the number
of completion—in her birthdate. God put His stamp of
completion on Deja' at birth.

Her father's family did not recognize Mia as someone
significant in their son's life, so they just discarded her.
Deja' never had a relationship with her father's family, and
since he had a big family, 11 brothers and sisters, she grew
up wondering if any man she dated could be her cousin or
other family member.

Mia told Deja' that her father died in the military, so she would not feel she was worthless and born to a 17-year-old girl involved with a guy who did not care about her, and who was a street guy and killed because of his deeds. Her life started off with a lie about someone whose DNA was a part of who Deja' would be.

Deja's mom, Mia, struggled so much with identity and wanting to be accepted and loved due to her own broken relationship with her mom that it led her down a path of selfishness and neglect towards her own child. Deja' entered this world with no father and a broken mom who was just 17. Mia was running the street, leaving Deja' bouncing from pillar to post, putting her in situations that no young girl should ever be put in.

Mia was running numbers and experimenting with drugs, a path that led to addiction and further abandonment of Deja'. So, no father and a mom who was caught up in the street—what a hand to be dealt!

God made moves, though. Although Deja' was going from pillar to post, there were people who made positive, life-changing investments in her, in the midst of those who molested her, threw her away, and wrote her off, determined she would amount to nothing just like her mom. Either it was the father of one of the pillars, the son of one of the posts, neighbors, or people in the community.

There were also family members or those Deja' trusted who touched or spoke to her inappropriately. Although she was subjected to these things, God was still working and did not let any of these things destroy her.

Yes, Deja' suffered and was in pain a lot of her childhood, but she continued to have a dream and envisioned herself as successful in life. Her favorite show was *Little House On the Prairie*, which gave her a sense of family, although it was a TV show. Deja' also had people on her journey that ushered her along.

How many of you can relate to this and put yourself in Deja's shoes with your own story, and go back and see how God was involved the whole time although you did not know it? Well, there was a grandmother, Alma, who was meek and prayerful. She trusted God and was able to share that with Deja' and it gave her strength.

Most people saw Alma as weak for the many mistakes she made in her own life early on, but she was strong in her belief in God's power to do anything, as He had kept her by His side and helped her through some really tough times in her life. This gave Deja' the belief that no matter what was going on, God would work it out. Thank God for Alma, because this helped Deja' not to give up.

We all have someone in our lives like that. What a blessing. Who was that for you?

There were also other people who helped Deja' on her journey. There was Teddy, her stepdad, who came into Mia's life when Deja' was two or three. He taught her how to be a lady and be feminine. Teddy was a caregiver; he made sure she bathed and had proper hygiene, that she had a meal to eat and knew how to dress properly. Although Mia was present and did give care, she was very inconsistent as a mom. In Deja's eyes, she was seen as ambitious and a fly girl.

Mia dressed really nicely, and had lots of friends who looked up to her. But that was Mia's priority and Deja' was not, and she always longed for Mia's love. However, Mia did, at an early age, give Deja' an example of leadership and mental strength. She would always buy her books to read. Encouraging reading is one of the best things you can do for a child. Once again, God was making moves.

Although Mia may have thought it was a way to get Deja' out of her face (at least this is what Deja' believed), she was actually building her mind.

Mia also sent Deja' away to summer camp for six weeks each year, which showed the young girl that there was more in the world than just the hood, or the block, or the local schoolyard.

No matter how much is bad, there is always some good. Remember that. Keep yourself in a place where nothing is wasted; take the good and throw away the bad. God does not waste anything, and neither should you.

There was also a godfather, James, who was a drug dealer and very street smart, who taught Deja' how to stand up for herself and know that she was special. He taught her how to command respect, respect herself, and to think for herself and be strong.

James would ask random math questions off the cuff, catching Deja' off guard, and if she answered correctly he would pull out a wad of money and give her a few dollars. He would give her riddles to figure out, and let her watch him interact with people, to show her how to talk to others and ask for what she wanted without fear. James taught Deja' that life was not fair, and that if she wanted anything in life, she would have to go get it without making excuses and fight for it if she had to.

Of course, Deja' was also able to see drug deals done, drugs being processed, guns, fights and lots of other negative things as well, but James always kept her focused on the positive.

He told Deja' she could be a lawyer because she asked lots of questions. He encouraged the good she could achieve, instead of glamorizing his lifestyle and what came with it.

I repeat, take the good and leave the bad, because being in this environment did cause Deja' to get shot at 12 years old. She was in the wrong place at the wrong time, receiving a wound that could have killed her—but it didn't.

She wore a cast from her hip to her toes for months, and was almost left back in seventh grade because of it. Deja' had to walk on crutches and get X-rays regularly to make sure the bullet did not move, as it was lodged between a bone and several nerves. It could not be removed without causing major damage, so to this day Deja' still has that bullet lodged in her bone.

Once the cast was removed, she had to go through lots of physical therapy to walk again. This was very hard for her, and people would make nicknames for Deja' like "peg leg" or "hopalong." Her mother Mia, however, was not light on the matter. Even with all her issues, she would sometimes take Deja's crutches and tell her to stop hopping and walk, because if she didn't, she would be hopping for the rest of her life. Deja', in pain and fear of falling, constantly tried to walk with full pressure on that leg and eventually was able to walk again.

Mia may not have been all things, but she was indeed a fighter, and made Deja' fight to walk.

There was also a godmother, Alice, unrelated to the godfather (that's how it is in the hood) but thank God for her. She lived in the same building as Mia and Deja', just a few floors down, and always would let Deja sleep at her house. She had two daughters, Debbie and Dawn, who were close to Deja's age, only a year apart.

Alice was a godsend; there were many days she found Deja' outside in front of the building, just sitting and waiting for Mia to come home, and it was after 11 PM most times. Alice would bring her in the house and put her to bed with her own daughters.

It got to the point where, if Alice did not see Deja' outside, she would go up to the floor she lived on and find her sitting at the door or on the hallway window ledge late at night, and take her downstairs, feed her, and put her to bed.

I'm sure you are wondering "Where is Teddy, the stepdad who was the caregiver earlier in the story?" Well, of course, he wasn't squeaky clean either, and by this point he was not around anymore to provide stability, as he had an argument with someone in the street and shot them, and was in jail serving five years. Another loss for Deja, and of course at such a young age, five years sounded like 50 years.

Eventually due to the drugs and the street life, Mia was evicted and did not know where she would go or what to do with Deja'. But God had it that this young girl, after the marshals locked them out with all their belongings still inside the house, was headed to her grandmother's house.

She begged her mom to stop at the Chinese restaurant on the corner as they were leaving. Who did they run into, but Alice, her godmother. When she found out they had been evicted, she asked Mia, "What are you going to do with the child?" Mia said she did not know. Alice said, "Well, since she goes to school down the street, and she and my girls are like sisters, let her stay with me at least until school is finished and you get a place." Mia said yes.

Look at God!

With no papers of legal guardianship, Alice was able to mother Deja' for several years. Mia visited, but was too far in the streets to consider taking Deja' so the young girl was raised by her godmother Alice. Mia visited periodically, and Deja' would spend time with her in the summers while also spending time with her grandmother, aunts and uncle.

Deja', Debbie and Dawn were close. Deja' was welcomed into the family as another sister. They were called the DDD sisters in the neighborhood. They went to the movies on the weekends and loved to go to the Sabrett frank shop to get hot dogs when they went shopping on Fulton Street in downtown Brooklyn. They didn't always have money to actually shop, but they window-shopped and it was a great getaway from the neighborhood.

They shared stories with each other and fought like cats and dogs, especially Deja' and Dawn, who were like twins. They looked alike and dressed alike. It's funny because people were convinced they were related by blood. Perhaps that was true, because they did all cut their fingers and rub them together to make it official, so they thought.

They shared many life experiences together, like first boyfriends, first heartbreaks, learning to ride the train and bus together. They loved to play outside and jump double dutch, play handball and race.

Going to New Jersey to visit family was a treat. They spent summers in Elizabeth, New Jersey and loved it. Although at times they fought, it was only because they had different personalities. Despite the arguments and fighting, they loved each other and took care of one another when any of them were sick or got hurt. They helped each other study for tests and celebrated each other's successes. They put up the tree together at Christmas and helped cook meals for Thanksgiving—well, Deja' and Dawn did. Cooking was not Debbie's strong suit. When Deja' got shot and wore a cast for several months, they each took turns with a wire hanger, sticking it inside the cast to scratch her itchy leg.

Alice was so involved in Deja's life that during that summer visit with Mia, when she got shot, Alice was ready to turn the hood upside down. When Deja' came home from the hospital, Alice came and got her in a cab because she did not drive and said, "She is coming home with me and I want someone to try to stop me!" As I stated earlier, she was a godsend.

Alice went to physical therapy with Deja along with Mia, and helped her adjust to school and life on crutches during those months. As I mentioned, Deja' was almost left back because the school did not have elevators; and she could not make it up and down several flights of steps daily. Thankfully there was a program called Gates, for kids who were technically left back due to poor grades. Although Deja' had good grades, she was able to participate because of her situation, and it was that which kept her from being left back.

Alice pushed Deja' to study hard for five months and take the test to advance. Deja passed, went on to eighth grade, and was able to graduate middle school on time with all her friends. Everyone needs support and Alice was definitely a support system for this young girl.

Alice did not have much by way of financial means, but did all she could as a single mother, raising three girls with their father living home sometimes but just as often not, until he was finally gone for good. She struggled financially to feed and clothe Debbie, Deja' and Dawn. They shared food often. Gravy and rice from the Chinese restaurant was a common meal, or four chicken wings and egg rolls, which was Deja's favorite. There were many days when they ate franks and beans or mayo sandwiches. But when Alice hit the number, it was like Christmas. They had sweet beef sausages from the meat market, the cabinets

and refrigerator were full of food, and each of the girls got
to order whatever they wanted, without having to share.

Food stamps were what carried them from month to
month, especially since there was another mouth to feed.
Alice could not get any assistance for Deja' without any
paperwork or legal guardianship. If she tried, the Bureau
of Child Welfare (BCW) would try to put Deja' in foster
care, as they had tried once before, due to a freak accident
when she accidentally got burned.

BCW made it known that they planned to take Deja',
although Alice begged them not to. Somehow, God
supernaturally worked it out, in that for some reason the
case worker never arrived to pick Deja' up, and they never
heard from BCW again. So Alice did her best, financially,
and worked it out without much help, except from Alma,
the grandmother, who did what she could.

She loved those three girls, and was a strict mom.
During the winter they had to be inside by the time the
streetlights came on. If you are over 40, and lived in New
York or up north, you for sure know what I mean. All
you heard was Alice's loud voice in front of the building
yelling, "Girls, girls, let's make it!" They knew what that
meant and, embarrassed or not, they made it!

Alice did her best to be a protector and made sure she
drilled family principles about decorum and morals into
their heads. They prayed together during times of struggle
and she would read encouraging scriptures to the girls
when they would complain about their lack of material
things. She would always encourage Deja' to walk with
her head up and not drag her feet, because even though
she did her best to mother this young girl, Deja' still knew
she was the extra child, having to wear hand-me-downs
and sometimes being treated differently by neighbors or

Alice's family members. She did not always feel equal as a daughter. Therefore she always longed for her own mother and was sad a lot of the time.

Deja's self-esteem was challenged, and she felt abandoned and alone. *Little House On the Prairie* was her way of visualizing the family she wanted, and she was able to live it through that TV show. Deja' had other coping methods that helped her maintain a since of stability and peace; even though it was fantasy-driven, it helped her maintain sanity and focus on the life she wanted, one she believed she could and would have.

She cherished the happy times of being able to run track, which was a dream of hers and was on TV, running for Pratt Institute. Once she got shot that was a dream denied, yet she enjoyed every moment of it when she was running.

She relished learning to tap dance, and performing in front of an audience of several hundred people wearing a fabulous sparkling costume and fishnet stockings. She was always the lead because she was so short, which forced her to work hard and perfect each move. It was a great experience.

She also loved to help her grandmother and Alice cook and especially bake cakes, because she loved to lick the spoon and the bowl once the batter went into the pan. She enjoyed having that quality time with Alma and Alice.

She also enjoyed times with Mia when she would teach her how to type on the typewriter and play dress-up with all her nice hats and shoes. Mia would show Deja off, letting her read any book one of her friends would take off the bookshelf. Deja' had every book memorized cover to cover, and could recite them word for word, page by page, without missing a word and without even looking at the book, all she needed was the title. Mia was amazed and praised Deja' to her friends for being smart.

The three girls grew up as sisters and loved each other. They protected one another and were a support system for one another over the years, standing together and sharing many memories when their mom, Alice, passed. That was a rough time for Debbie, Deja' and Dawn, because Alice was their anchor, their cheerleader, their course corrector and source of encouragement. During Alice's last days and months they took turns caring for her and showing her as much love and appreciation as they could. It's always too soon to lose someone you love and respect. The DDD girls are still sisters to this day, which proves it's not always about blood.

Chapter Two
Deja' Today

Let me pause for a moment and give you a present-day look at Deja', who is now a 46-year-old woman. Then I'll take you further into the journey she underwent to arrive at this point.

I wanted to let you see her beginnings first, though of course I will not be able to tell you the end in this book as her life is still being written.

Today, Deja' lives in North Carolina, a long way away from her beginnings in Brooklyn. She lives in a nice gated community that she loves, is a bank manager and currently owns five investment properties where she collects rent from tenants. Deja' has a plan to flip houses over the next few years, and then move on to buying five more properties and retiring. She attends World Overcomers Christian Church in Durham, and loves living in NC. She also has continued each Sunday to live stream services from the church that played a large part in her spiritual growth over the years, Christian Cultural Center in Brooklyn, NY.

A few years ago, Deja' was able to purchase one of her dream cars, a Lexus RX350. She loves driving it and was proud to buy it brand new. She is even more excited to have paid it off early, while it's still practically new.

She is fairly tight with her money, as being broke for many years taught her that what you do with your money can make you rich or poor. The tangible things are not as important as the intangible ones like financial freedom from a job, residual income, positioning yourself to be able to help your mom in her later years, and not being confounded by time constraints, a job, or financial pressures.

Deja' will, however, splurge on vacations as she loves to take all-inclusive trips out of the country with no sparing on pampering at the best resorts she can find. She also likes to take her mother Mia on trips and do nice things for her as often as she can. She enjoys sitting out on the balcony in the mornings with a hot cup of tea or cocoa and listening to the birds chirp while she thinks about life. During the summer she will sit out there in the evening with a glass of wine and some music. Deja' also likes to go out to dinner and have a spa day in her free time. Other than that, she puts her finances in to building her vision and her dream.

Deja keeps a date every Sunday with her girlfriends Toni and Gill from high school. They live in different states, but each committed to not let distance break them apart. They travel together on lavish trips once a year, and try to have periodic weekend visits also. They laugh together, cry together, and keep each other up to date on life events both good and bad. They also call one another on the carpet from time to time, saying, "OK, chick, get it together," when they need to.

They often reminisce when they get together about high school and other events they've shared, and still act like they are in their twenties at times. They listen to old hip-hop and R&B music over a few drinks and fried porgies. They play cards and try to do some of the old dances from back in the days. They are a mess when they get together! Their families admire their friendship and comment about how it is so rare for friends to remain so close for so many years, especially when living in different states.

Deja' and Tyra, her girlfriend since the age of 10, are like sisters and have shared many struggles and victories together. Their lives were similar in some regards, yet different in so many ways. They both struggled financially during their young years but had dreams of success. They are able to look back on their late teens and early twenties with gratitude for some of the choices they made that allowed them to fulfill many of those dreams. Tyra married Steven, a great guy who did not shy away from being a young dad and made the choice to work hard supporting her and their family when they were barely twenty years old themselves. They are still happily married today after raising three great children together.

Today, Deja' and Tyra still speak regularly and are amazed by how each of her three children, Deja's godchildren, grew up so fast, graduated college. Two are now married—my, how time does fly.

They are both still chasing their dreams, and encourage one another every step of the way. They celebrate each other's successes and at other times give advice. Living in different states does not allow Deja' to attend every event but there was FaceTime that showed the wedding dress being picked out and the new home when the oldest daughter moved out, all live streamed on video. She travels to New York to attend special events like engagement parties and weddings. Tyra does it all with class and elegance. She spares no kindness in making Deja comfortable when she visits; it's almost like she is staying in a resort. They are truly besties for life.

When Deja' moved to North Carolina, she was placed in a financial center that needed a lot of work to win in sales and achieve operational soundness. Deja took on the challenge and has worked to assemble a team that wants to win. Together they were able to be successful each quarter and celebrate.

Deja' takes pride in strategizing and executing to create success. She is proud of her team for working hard. She tries her best to create a work/life balance where associates not only work hard, but laugh hard, and come to work feeling they are a part of something great without having to neglect their families' needs. It's a juggling act at times, but she truly feels it's the right thing to do.

Deja is of the opinion that they have goals to hit, and people who count on them to win, and they do not have the luxury of losing sight of that even for a moment, yet at the same time family is equally important and parents, children, and spouses are also priorities in the lives of each associate.

Deja' works hard to prepare her staff to do great things and be ready for promotions and opportunities. She often smiles when she reconnects with people who have moved on or even those who left the company for other opportunities. Some of them say that they often share with their peers that Deja' was the best manager they've had. They state that she was hard on them, and at the time they felt she was being "extra," but came to realize she really cared about them as people as well as their careers, and took time to teach them how to do better and be better in life, inside and outside the workplace.

Deja's team has a funny saying in their center: "if you can work here, you can work anywhere," because you learn what's important, why it's important, and the value you bring to every aspect of the center running successfully, regardless of your role.

Deja' once received a card from an associate she hired who had moved on into a new role as a result of a promotion. The card said, in summary, I interviewed with several other managers in the company locally and in other states but you were the one who saw something in me and gave me a shot. That person is a manager in the company today and started with Deja' as a teller just a few years earlier.

Deja's supervisor once told her that she may not realize the power of influence she has, and that anyone who does not grow under her leadership was simply not willing.

Deja' attributes her successes in life to all of her experiences collectively, both good and bad. Most importantly, she believes it's not what happens to you but how you respond to what happens to you. That may sound clichéd but it is actually true. If one person made it through a situation, then so can you. Attitude determines altitude. Your attitude determines approach and approach determines success or failure.

When Deja' experiences hardships or setbacks, her rule of thumb is generally to analyze: what's happening? How did it happen? And what part did she play in it happening? She believes this helps remove the emotion from the event and put you in a position to be accountable. You then are better equipped to come up with a solution, soundly and quickly.

Emotions are what cause delay in reasoning. You reject the possibility of it being your fault, even in part, or you spend too much time having a pity party. Although you need to have a pity party sometimes, make sure it is brief, then move on. If you take too much time being concerned about it being someone else's fault, you don't shift your thinking to solutions, which is what it takes to grow, develop and achieve success.

Another extremely important exercise Deja' reminds herself of is what it takes to have courage. There are situations in life that can paralyze you if you let fear set in. You will talk yourself right out of a blessing on account of fear. Deja' once read a book called *Feel the Fear and Do It Anyway*. It's like the acronym FEAR (False Evidence Appearing Real); instead, she exercises FAITH (Feel As If the Thing has Happened), applying it to what you want to see happen. Place your energy and focus on that instead, that's when courage steps forward and fear takes a back seat.

Finally, the other factor Deja' attributes her success to is her thought and prayer life. She trusts God and does not put too much thought into naysayers. She knows that God will love you with the evidence while people will hate you on speculation. So if you make a mistake, don't let others judge you, give it to Him and keep moving forward. The quality of your thinking determines the quality of your life; garbage in, garbage out, so filter what you let in to your thought life. Take the time to plan, strategize and know what you want.

Deja' believes in herself and sets her sights on her dreams by continuing to live each day with determination, faith, discipline, and love for herself and others. She prays for discernment, and the ability to look beyond the obvious and to always believe in miracles, which are God intervening into human affairs. Discipline is the bridge between preparation and accomplishment, therefore you can play now and pay later or pay now and play for the rest of your life.

Chapter Three
The Launch Pad

Deja' had a strong building block that was like a launch pad: at age 21, she became a corrections officer in the men's prison at Rikers Island, and did that job for ten years, earning six figures a year with lots of overtime. She was not afraid of hard work and was proud of her achievements. No more franks and beans, hand-me-down clothes, home perms making her hair fall out, or living in a constant state of being broke.

Being a corrections officer, however, is not a job for the weary or the heartless. You have a responsibility for people's lives on both sides. You are responsible for your partner as well as each inmate you are maintaining custody of.

Life in prison had its good and bad days. For the officer you had to have mental and emotional strength to lead and keep order. Generally it could be one inmate in your care you are escorting, 50 to 100 in a housing area with a partner, or several hundred at a time in the yard or mess hall with only 8 to 10 officers controlling movement. This required you to take your training seriously, always be alert and follow procedures, because lives depended on it.

There were also times you were able to speak into the lives of the men who were incarcerated giving encouragement and words of wisdom. Deja' has encountered many inmates in the outside world after their release; generally the encounter would begin by hearing a voice from a car or on the street yelling, "Hey C.O."

For an instant, she would be nervous, as she had all sorts of experiences with inmates inside. Some had to be corrected for breaking rules, or were just mad that the lights went out for the night or about having to get off the phone when their time was over. But each time the ex-inmate would say, "I had mad respect for you, you were always fair." Some would even apologize for being disrespectful.

They would share times that Deja' helped them with encouraging words after a not-so-pleasant visit with family or a court date gone bad. They even reminded her of times she talked them out of doing something stupid out of rage and anger that could have caused them to get another charge, and more time; but instead now they are home, doing well, and plan to never go back.

Deja' always walked away from those encounters thinking, "That is why you should always treat people with respect, because only God is their judge and jury." There are many men and women who made poor choices that landed them in prison, doing short time or long stretches of time, who wished they could have made a different choice. Many of them are talented in that they can sing, rap, draw, paint, write and do so much more. Nevertheless, there also were, in the midst of those who had regrets and were talented, those who were violent, manipulative and dangerous.

Each inmate was not the same, therefore for the violent and manipulative ones you could not be weary, you had to stand your ground and maintain order and safety at all times while also giving respect and honoring their rights. For those who were not violent and followed prison protocol without issue, you could not be heartless either, but instead make every effort to treat them with respect, allowing them their dignity as men.

For the purposes of clarity, I am not speaking of favoritism, I am speaking of differentiation. If one prisoner violated a rule, another prisoner should not be subjected to the consequence of the one who violated just because they lived in the same housing area. There is no room for preferential treatment, only fair treatment. Preferential treatment can cause an officer or an inmate to get hurt or killed. There are many officers who were examples of fathers, mothers and mentors to these men, both young and older, based on how the officers conducted themselves. There are also officers who saw that shield as representative of family and stood with and for one other in support, partnership and respect for the job that needed to be done daily.

Each officer undertakes a lot in that they have family and life challenges of their own, yet they put on that uniform each day to go inside a prison where they are not sure of what the day will bring, but manage to keep a level head and emotional control and maintain safety, while delivering care, custody and control in sometimes rough and dangerous situations. Like police officers, correction officers have to run toward dangerous situations instead of run from them, and that takes courage.

Deja' was proud to be an officer and respects those who work in the prison system because the outside world, at times, tends to think their jobs are easy and considers them babysitters, instead of the ones who have to maintain order and control over all the people the outside world called 911 about, and now they are all gathered together in one place, prison, with corrections officers!

Being a corrections officer also provided a financial foundation for Deja' and allowed her the freedom to dream bigger. She developed leadership, partnership and courage in that position. However, there are stepping stones in our lives that are there to be launch pads not anchor places. We may not fully understand at the time but there are usually events that occur in our lives that usher us in and out of seasons. We just have to try to respond at the correct times, not too earlier and not too late. However, sometimes that can be a bit tricky.

Fate had it that Alma, her grandmother whose caregiver she had become, would pass, and it propelled her to move to North Carolina. Deja' was destined to move to the South, but how would she get there when retiring from corrections would have been the natural path of progression?

Even when you do not know what you are doing, God is working behind the scenes. You know sometimes God will tell you or show you a glimpse of your future, but you see it as your right now based on your current situation, so you move on it. Deja' remembers hearing someone once say, "We make bad choices based on not having enough information or our lack of understanding of the information we have."

God has a plan for your life that's unknown to you. It's about time and timing though, as long as you are moving he will align the stars, even if you jump the gun like Deja' did.

Deja' took her 401k and moved to North Carolina and lived on that for seven months. She was in a deep state of grief after losing her grandmother, but believe it or not, those seven months of alone time were just what she needed to recover. When you are the caregiver and someone passes, although it was out of your control you still go through the stages of grief. One of those stages is guilt. Deja' wondered if there was something she could have done differently and was weighed down with the thought that she might have missed something.

She changed her shift at work and started working two days of 16-hour shifts to be off four days in a row, allowing her to be there to care for Alma, yet on one of her two working days she received the call from the hospital that her grandmother had passed. She felt guilty for not being there in those final moments and it literally took the wind out of her sails. During the seven months of recovery time, Deja' did not know what she would do afterward; all she knew was, Lord, as long as you are here with me, you will make a way.

She was criticized for leaving corrections after 10 years with good pay, benefits, and a retirement plan, and not having full clarity about her future. All she knew was that her peace of mind and her trust in God were all she needed. There were many people trying to convince her not to go. Badgering her with questions like, "Why are you giving up your whole life? You are making a huge mistake." Deja', while struggling with all the feedback, was in a bad place emotionally and barely able to think straight. All she could hear inside while she was trying to make sense of what direction her life was now going was, *If you do not get your peace back you are going to spiral out of control.*

She launched into the deep after doing some calculations of best-case and worst-case scenarios, and there she was in North Carolina, on faith, and what she was able to take from her 401k.

After seven months, Deja' was ready to get up and move. She was involved in a network marketing business that helped keep her in an advent reading mode: people skills books, leadership books and spiritual books. This continued to help build her and guide her.

Deja's up-line was supportive and encouraged her to build her business, but being away from her team and immediate sponsor was a struggle of sorts. Deja' would need to build a new team, and contend with the fact that her immediate sponsor, who was her greatest strength to build, was also a point of pain in that they had dated for years before he betrayed her and broke her heart. How could she build in that situation? But it's all in the cards.

Deja' got a job as a teller at a bank. It represented a significant pay cut, but she did it with a positive attitude. After two years, she decided to move back to New York.

Deja' had been looked at as having made a mistake for leaving New York. Then she got a job paying half what she'd made working corrections, and now she was returning to New York. All roads pointed to Deja' being a failure.

Something worth noting: Don't ever let failure make you stuck! Try, fail, adjust. Some people encouraged Deja', while others talked about her behind her back as they smiled in her face, claiming to be friends. Deja reached out to Monica, a friend from corrections, and shared what she intended to do. Deja and Monica were close during her years as a corrections officer. They were like each other's shadow. When you saw one you saw the other. They did everything together and had a blast doing a lot of fun and sometimes crazy things together. While Deja was married their husbands became friends also, and together they traveled and spent time at one another's house often. Deja and Monica hung out on weekends, gave each other advice, shared life's challenges together and always supported one another. They stayed in touch even after Deja moved to North Carolina. When Deja called Monica informing her she wanted to return to New York, Monica immediately said, "come stay with me for as long as you need to". So, for a few months, until she found her own place, Deja stayed in Monica's fully furnished, finished basement. It was like a suite and very nice. Monica went out of her way to make sure Deja was comfortable during her stay. Deja was grateful to have that support while she struggled to start over and they are still friends and keep in touch to this day.

As I shared a few paragraphs ago, God knows what He is doing, and as long as you are moving, He is guiding. Thank you Jesus!

Deja could have gone back to corrections, since there was a window of a few years during which she could return without starting over with the academy and the test, but that season of her life was over. Deja' had gotten what she needed from corrections, and if she had gone in that direction it would have taken her life backwards. Deja' instead decided to continue with banking in New York.

Can you imagine what the naysayers were saying during this time? OMG! But Deja' knew who she was and had already experienced many setbacks in life, yet always had full confidence that she was going to win and this was all happening for a reason. If God had brought her through her childhood with all its heartaches and pain, then this was just part of a bigger picture, she reasoned.

Deja' applied for a teller's position, and was hired for a teller/seller's position instead. This position was in a location they called a Denovo. Each associate sold products, opened checking and savings accounts, had their life and health licenses to sell insurance, and managed all aspects of mortgages, from application to closing. She also handled deposits, withdrawals and payments for customers. Each associate was trained to function in several capacities that are, in today's banking industry, delegated to separate roles and departments. After only a year and a half, she was offered an assistant manager's position. While excited about this, and feeling like things were going in the right direction, Deja' still had some distance to go to get back to her corrections salary.

Deja' met a woman named Terry during the assistant manager training class and they became friends. People you meet and relationships you build are very important parts of your journey! People are placed in your life, sometimes for brief periods, to serve a purpose in your life, or for you to serve a purpose in theirs. It may only be for a season and then you never see them again, but relationships are doorways, so value them.

Terry ended up leaving the bank, and when she did, she called Deja' from her next employer, saying, "You should come over here—they will appreciate your skill set, and the pay is much better."

Deja' applied for an assistant manager's position, since that was the new role she was training for. She took the test, and when the bank's hiring manager called her, she said, "We are not sure if you applied for the assistant manager role by mistake, but based on your test results, we believe you are a better fit for a branch manager's role."

Deja' was shocked, excited and terrified all at the same time. A little over a year ago she had been a teller. She thought, *I decided to make the move back to New York, feeling unsure if I'd made a mistake moving to North Carolina, giving up a "good job" and unsure if I'd made a mistake returning to New York, and now look at this. Wow!*

Deja' went forward and interviewed with the market manager, and was hired as the branch manager for a banking center in Queens. Hence the saying, God can do exceedingly and abundantly more than you can ask or think, and it gets better; pressed down, shaken together, and running over, He causes people to pour into your lap.

Deja' ran the center very well, taking it from low-performing to a top performer and even winning an all-expense-paid trip for two to a wonderful resort in Scottsdale, Arizona. But remember, the glimpse of her destiny was that she would end up in the south. So after about a year, Deja' started thinking about moving back to North Carolina—but for the right reasons this time, not because of mourning, but because now she had a point of comparison that let her see a different lifestyle and level of comfort.

She had to go on that first journey to North Carolina on faith and be seen as crazy and a failure because her destiny was attached to it. She had learned that God, not her job, was her provider. But now, Deja' was doing great in her job and was even back to the six-figure salary she thought she'd lost—she was now getting paid more than she had in corrections.

Look to God! Stay true to yourself and have a few anchors that are not negotiable, like peace of mind. First and foremost, know that all things work together for good, although they are all not good. Listen to your true self no matter what others say.

Make moves, even when in doubt, by counting the cost and being willing to fight and pay the price for your decisions. Otherwise you will be paying a price for someone else's decisions that you let influence you to do what they thought you should do. I will also add that many times people suggest things that they themselves wouldn't do. So go within and count the cost and go for it based on faith because God honors faith even if you make wrong choices at times.

Deja started looking for managerial positions in North Carolina. Friends suggested she go back to Fayetteville, but that was not in the plan.

A position became available in Raleigh. She had never been to Raleigh, nor did she know anyone there. She would have to take a significant pay cut to go, but when the cost of living was compared, her salary would be enough that she could live like she had in New York.

Deja' was determined to get back over six figures anyway, because God was her source, not any particular job. Her experience strengthened her faith and that pay cut was not as important as it would have been to other people.

Deja' interviewed over the phone with the market manager in Raleigh and was offered the position on the spot. She had to say, let me think about it for a day and get back to you.

When blessings come, you are not really surprised, because you are in faith and believing that whatever you put your hand to will prosper—still, just how fast it happens can amaze you, in a good way.

Deja' accepted the job, packed up a truck, and off she went to a city she had never been to and where she did not know a soul or how to get around, but she was excited and this time had a passion and the goal of never looking back.

Almost ten years later, this is her home, and God has done some amazing things in her life that she knows would never have happened if she stayed in New York. Deja' knows she would not have the calm, quiet and peaceful life she currently enjoys nor would she have five investment properties as a residual income stream. As this book is being written, she is currently developing an online course that has the potential to help thousands of people overcome life's challenges and will be specifically covering topics such as abandonment, "the warrior in the mirror," and others. To God be the glory!

Chapter Four
Healing and Restoration

After many years, Deja's mother Mia got sober and married a man named David, who loved her dearly. David was there through many of the years Mia struggled with addiction. If you have had family or a spouse battle with addiction you know the challenges firsthand. You are in constant fear of them being hurt or overdosing. They generally are manipulative and you find yourself trying to protect yourself from them pulling a fast one on you, while also trying to protect them from their own reckless behaviors.

David had his own run with addiction long before, and had been sober for many years, so although he was fairly equipped for the challenges, it wore him out as well. He was committed to Mia and loved her through it all. He defended her on every front and continuously tried to get her sober. He even stood up for her to his family who at times felt she was using him. He knew she was sick, just as he had been sick in his past life. God knows what you need and sends the right people who he strengthens to help bring you out.

After many years of supporting Mia, David came to a breaking point. He had retired from NYC Transit authority as a motorman after 30 years and decided he wanted to move back to his hometown in Virginia. He gave Mia an ultimatum which she squandered, and David found himself telling her he was done. He was tired!

This day was, I'm sure, a heart-wrenching one for David, as he loved Mia and only wanted the best for her. He told her she had to leave. Mia called Deja', crying on the phone saying, "He is kicking me out. Deja was headed to work, as she was still a corrections officer at the time. It was a Friday and she knew she had to step in or her mom would be lost forever with David now throwing in the towel. She begged David to let Mia stay until Monday and she would come get her. Deja' arranged to be off that Monday and over the weekend did as much research as she could to find a long-term detox facility for her mom.

She knew all the other short-term facilities had never helped and this time something more drastic needed to be done. She found a place, Samaritan Village, that had excellent results and called them to arrange for them to help Mia.

This time, Mia had no choice but to take the offer that she had refused in the past. That Monday morning, Deja' picked Mia up and took her to the facility. As you can imagine, it was a rough and emotional day for both of them. She checked Mia in and prayed this would work this time.

During the first few days, which is the initial phase of the program before each candidate is transferred to the long-term facility, Deja' received information that the long-term care facility was full and they would only be able to give short-term care for 14 days.

Deja' was devastated and asked to speak to the director. She sat in front of the director with tears in her eyes, sharing with him the journey of finally getting here. She explained that this was the only shot Mia had that could actually work. She begged him to find a slot.

He told Deja' he would see what he could do, but not to have high hopes because the program was very strict about occupancy.

That day Deja' prayed asking God to make a way because she wanted her mother to live and not die. She was terrified and pleading with God to touch the heart of the director and move him to find a slot.

The next day when she visited, one of the caregivers told Deja' the director wanted to see her when she arrived. Deja' was quietly whispering inside, "Please God, let him have found a slot." With her nerves standing on end, she entered his office.

The words that came from a miracle performed flowed from his mouth: "We found a slot, your mom can stay." Deja was elated and the director, with tears in his eyes embraced this young woman who fell in his arms, crying intensely with tears of joy and relief, thanking him and telling him she was praying so hard. As he held her, he said, "God answered your prayers, she's going to be OK."

David was in close communication with Deja' as he was hoping she would be able to help Mia. With the good news in hand she told David Mia was accepted into long-term care, nine months of being on a structured recovery plan. David said, "If she gets sober, I want her to come join me in Virginia and I will marry her."

God has a good sense of humor. He has greater plans for you than you can imagine, despite your past or your present destructive behaviors, he just has to get you in the right position to receive them. Deja' shared this news with Mia and she was shocked, because she thought David did not love her anymore.

David moved to Virginia and built a home on land he owned. He spoke to Mia regularly over the phone and received updates from Deja' over the months of treatment.

If you can hear the *Rocky* theme song in your head, from when he was training and struggling to prepare to fight Apollo Creed, that's what was going on with Mia. She had good and bad days. Some days she wanted to give up, but Deja' was there giving her encouraging words and visiting regularly.

Mia's mom and sisters and brother visited also, sharing stories of how they admired her so much before she was overcome by the street. How she was always fly and popular and had her own place at such a young age. They shared how they looked up to her because, although she didn't keep jobs because of her life in the street, she was so smart and always had good jobs with the city and had been able to ace the tests without even studying.

Mia was surprised to hear that she was a role model to her siblings and was sorry she let them down. She was especially sorry for not being there for Deja'. They embraced and everyone told Mia they forgave her and only wanted to see her sober and living a happy, healthy life.

Of course, the enemy was looming. One day, after Mia had been there for several months, she had an encounter with one of the workers and it escalated into an argument. Mia said she was leaving, and she did!

Deja' received a call from the facility that sunk her heart. Mia was almost finished with the program, how could this happen? Note: when you are on your way to greatness the enemy is waiting for an opportunity to derail you, so always be on guard to defend your victory. When Deja' received this call and had not heard from Mia, she had the whole family on alert looking for her and waiting for a call. No one heard from Mia for the entire afternoon.

That evening, Deja' received a call from her aunt Erica, who said, "Mia just showed up at Mommy's house," referring to Deja's grandmother.

Deja' was now in damage control mode, because she knew the facility was strict and they had made it clear that once you leave, you cannot return, therefore that was not an option. She put a plan together to have the family keep eyes on Mia and not let her out of their sight. The next morning, she was going to put Mia on a bus to Virginia whether she wanted to go or not, because she was determined to save her mother's life. She spoke to David and told him about the argument and Mia leaving. He agreed to meet Mia at the Port Authority in Virginia.

That morning, Erica took Mia to the Port Authority in New York, and Deja' met them there. She purchased a ticket and they put Mia on the bus. This was not ideal, because the bus had a layover in DC and Mia was already upset and felt they were dictating her life and treating her like a prisoner.

Deja' was afraid Mia might get off the bus in DC and not make the full trip. She counted the hours and nervously considered the layover. She shared her concerns with David and he encouraged Deja' not to worry. Deja' received a call a few hours later from David but it was sooner than Mia was supposed to arrive in Virginia, so she panicked when she saw his name show up on the phone.

When she answered he said, "I got her."

Confused, Deja' said, "Her bus is not arriving for another two hours."

He said, "I decided to drive to DC to meet the bus for the layover." He further said that when the bus arrived he was standing waiting and Mia got off the bus and was shocked to see him. "When a man loves a woman, there is nothing he will not do for her." He embraced her and said, welcome home. A few months later, David and Mia married and her life was changed forever.

David was like a father figure to this now-grown woman. He was a roaring lion on the outside and a teddy bear on the inside. He pulled no punches when putting you in your place and telling his truth. One of his favorite lines was, "You need to learn to listen and listen to learn."

David also would do almost anything for you, so to know him was to love him. Deja' admired and loved him dearly, and was most honored by the care and protection he gave to Mia. She was eternally grateful to have a father figure like David, a man who loved and helped save her mother's life.

Who knew God would fix it that she would be blessed with four father figures in her life? Deja' would do anything for David. They had their challenges, in that David was a dominating man and no matter how grown you were, you were still treated like a child at times. He had a wealth of knowledge and lots of experiences to share, but at times you could not receive it because of his dominance. There were struggles in communication, but Deja' and David eventually became two peas in a pod.

They talked on the phone regularly, as he would call her in the mornings on her way to work. He was always up to date with current events and liked to share his worldview, so he and Deja' would sometimes be on the phone for hours talking about different topics.

Deja' would visit and get lessons on changing tires and other important things she needed to know about her car. She watched football games with him, and both he and

Deja' would have long talks in the car while waiting in the mall parking lot as Mia shopped. Mia loved to shop and neither David or Deja' had any interest in walking around the mall except for when she was finished—they would go inside to go to the food court and eat together.

David had two daughters, Yolanda and Shanice, who were like her godsisters; the three girls were close in age. Yolanda and Shanice were close with David and would visit also.

Like many blended families, they had their challenges with accepting one another and understanding one another's personalities and motives, especially since they were all grown by this time, but they got along and loved each other. They would get together during visits and cook and watch movies.

Yolanda was a fabulous dancer and excellent in her craft, so they would watch performances she did. Each of the girls had strong faith and would often talk about what God had done in their lives and how grateful they were. Shanice was the explorer and liked to have fun and do exciting things. She was also wise in her own right and was able to share wisdom and give advice. She was a supervisor for a government agency and was always strategizing and preparing for meetings. She was dedicated to being and doing her best.

One day they received news that David had a terminal illness, and everyone was shocked and hurt. Everyone came together in prayer and commitment to support him on this journey. Mia of course had the hardest undertaking. She was ready, though; God had prepared her as he caused David to invest in his own future returns during those rough years supporting Mia.

Mia was there every step of the way and did what a loving, committed wife would do. God saved Mia and now she was in a position to love and support a husband at a time he needed it most, with all she had in her. Doctor's appointments, bathing him, dressing him, leaves of absence from work to care for him. 911 calls to rush him to the hospital in the middle of the night, feeding him, getting help from nearby family and hiring extra help to care for him while she was at work: she did it all. She was praised by doctors for the level of care and attention she gave to David.

The girls came to support, lighten the load for Mia, encourage their dad, and go to doctor's appointments with David. Deja' took leaves of absence to give Mia and David as much support as she could. She would stay at the hospital for days with an overnight bag and give Mia the opportunity to go home, shower and sleep in her own bed some nights.

This journey took several years, as David was a fighter and pushed himself daily to enjoy as many healthy days as possible. Mia and David shared stories about their lives and all the struggles and happy times they'd enjoyed.

David had a cousin Carl who was like a brother (sadly while this book is being written Carl passed away. A loss for all who knew him). He visited often and had a standing phone call with David each morning. Even while David was sick, he was an integral part of forming a family estate with Carl. They planned together and had meetings with the county, and figured out ways to raise funds to stabilize the estate, like selling timber. By this time David was in a wheelchair and had more bad days than good, but his mind was still strong.

Mia was concerned, but would always host the family meetings, supplying breakfast and frying fish for lunch. She served David and made every effort to ease his pain and give him whatever he needed from her. Other family members came by to visit and called to offer encouragement.

When David passed, it was very hard for the girls and especially Mia. The girls helped make the arrangements for the home going services and tried to be there as a support for Mia as much as they could. Deja' took a leave of absence to spend time with her mom and help her adjust to life without David. Mia and David did everything together; she had lost her best friend.

Mia, however, pressed forward and keeps David alive in her heart. She and Deja' often joke and imitate some of his behaviors and sayings. During times of bad weather or days with car issues, they always remember how prepared he was for things like that and continue to follow what they think he would do and say if he were there.

David will always be remembered and loved by Mia and others. Mia often says she is happily single because she had a husband who loved, cherished and took care of her and she does not believe there is another who could fill his shoes.

Mia continues to have love and support. Deja' visits regularly and talks to Mia on the phone almost daily. They attend events together and Deja' takes her on trips and weekend getaways. God used David, through his commitment and love for Mia, to preserve the restoration and healing that was to come between Mia and Deja' years later, and used Deja' to mend the break that almost changed David and Mia's life many years ago, allowing for restoration, marriage and many happy years together that could potentially have been lost.

Although several years have passed, Yolanda and Shanice continue to check on Mia. They send cards and flowers for her birthday and Mother's Day. They call to wish her a Merry Christmas and Happy Thanksgiving, along with periodic calls to just say hello.

Once Deja' and Mia reconciled they became thick as thieves. They are so close that many are amazed and envious at times. God is so good that Mia looks younger than Deja', and if you did not know her, you would never know Mia was overcome by the street, used drugs heavily and was incarcerated. This goes to show that God can snatch you from darkness and still have time to restore all that was taken away from someone else who means the world to you, just so He can show His healing and restorative power.

Deja' married in the '90s and divorced in the 2000s with no children. She is open and honest that her choices in men were not one of her strong suits. Nonetheless, although she has had her challenges with love relationships, she is not bitter, nor has it minimized her self-worth or value. Her experiences have not caused her to think less of men as a whole. She believes there are still great men out there who have integrity, are loyal, honest, and faithful, who love God, can love and respect her, and are not intimidated by her independence, strong will, honesty and someone who will hold them accountable.

These broken relationships brought pain to Deja', yet she is not bitter or resentful. Instead, she is confident, knowing that each of these men simply did not recognize her value until after their betrayals, and abuse of her love, and ultimately it was their loss.

Deja' wants to be married again, and not necessarily to have children, but she would like a man who loves God, has street smarts and loves, honors and cherishes her. If she does not encounter such a man, she is also comfortable with her singleness. A great man would be an addition to her life, not the completion of it. A man is not required for joy and happiness, as she enjoys her own company. He will, however, be someone she can share her joy and happiness with.

Chapter Five
The Journey of Escape

Now back to Deja's journey as a young girl living out her process and determined to achieve her destiny.

I have taken you a million miles away from that broken, damaged, lost little girl, but I wanted you to see where your life can go even when it starts off looking like a losing hand.

It was definitely not easy, as a lot of the time Deja' could not trace God consciously. She just kept moving and trying to learn how to navigate her life with the hand she was dealt. Make no mistake, there were lots of lessons to learn and some courses unfortunately had to be repeated a few times, and some are still being repeated. Always be able to be a student, knowing that Graduation Day will come when you are six feet under in a box. Thank God for grace and mercy.

So what do you do when you have been molested, touched or talked dirty to by men over and over again throughout your childhood, and now you are in a safe place, in a home with a family because you had a godmother take you in, cover and nurture you for four years, yet you now find this thing raising its ugly head again at the hands of her man? Deja' thinks, *What is it about me that causes men to want to take advantage of me sexually? Is it because I don't have parents? Is it because I am a throwaway?* She's confused, finding herself in this position again after thinking she had been saved from all of that.

So, what do you do? Well, this had been the most stable home Deja' had been in, and living there had provided her with the longest amount of time without being subjected to sexual advances. She did not want to start any trouble, so she kept quiet and endured it. Alice, her godmother, did not know.

In fact this truth did not come out until Deja' was grown and married. The man had been dead for several years, yet for some reason she never told anyone what had happened.

Alice was devastated, crying and saying over and over again while embracing Deja', now a grown woman, "Why didn't you say anything? No man, and I mean no man, comes before my kids!" But how could Deja' have known that at the time? When she had tried to tell on other occasions in her life, she had not been believed.

After that period, and even after he had moved out, being in that house was always a reminder, but it was a secret that only Deja' knew about.

Life and secrets—what do you need to get free from? Secret fears, past abuses, abandonment, trust issues? What? Name it! Put a title to it and release it out into the atmosphere. Ask God to help you heal.

Life continues, and at 15 Deja' met and started dating Rick, a guy who had a stable or rather more stable family than she had experienced. Rick had both parents at home, with a mom who was a true matriarch and a dad who was a quiet and gentle man.

Vi cooked daily and had family dinner on Sundays where the whole family of brothers, sisters, grandchildren and friends would come over and be welcomed like family. This was the closest to *Little House On the Prairie* that Deja' could imagine.

At 17, Deja' went to Alice and asked if she could move in with Rick. Alice reluctantly said yes.

I believe that once Deja' poured her heart out to Alice, expressing how she had never felt as loved as she did by Rick and his family, and that he loved her and they would eventually get married, she felt compassion for her.

Still, Alice said it wasn't good for a young woman to live with a man, and that Deja' should stay on course to go to college, and could still date Rick without living with him. Deja' was adamant, and argued that Alice would not have to worry about taking care of her anymore, and that she did not want to live there anymore and was unhappy there.

I believe Alice eventually agreed because she wanted to do something to make Deja' happy after all she had been through. Alice knew it was not the best situation, but Deja's life was not ordinary so she could not treat it as ordinary.

Alice helped Deja' pack, and through tears and after periodic attempts to change the young girl's mind, she released Deja' and told her to stay strong, trust God and know that she could come back if she needed to.

To this day, Deja' knows that decision was hard for Alice to make, and went against everything in her, but she's grateful to Alice because it shaped so much of Deja's life to have that relationship and family.

Now since this book is about reality, meaning the real world, you know that all was not roses, right? Well, it was a loving relationship and the family support was awesome. They were a tight family who sacrificed for one another and were there for each other no matter what. Deja', who had experienced betrayal so often, was now experiencing immeasurable levels of support.

Deja' did go on to college, and went away to school instead of attending locally. This opened her up to experiences she had never had and gave her a sense of independence.

Deja' was excited to be on her own and away going after her dreams. She worked on campus at the cafeteria and even bought a life insurance policy. Deja' was ahead of her time and was frequently told she was an old soul and more advanced than most people her age. She was ambitious and determined to make something of herself.

Deja' was able to get good grades and planned to be an accountant so she could open her own firm and do taxes for large corporations. She had confidence and high self-esteem and took great pride in herself.

Let me pause for a moment, while you are feeling happy for Deja' or thinking that she was on her way. Did she heal? Did she ever address her pains? Nope; she buried them.

When pains are not healed, they have a tendency to be recycled and repeated. You know the phrase "deer in the headlights"—do you have the picture? Good.

Deja', now 19, came home from college to visit and found that Rick, who she loved so much, was cheating. She was devastated.

Rick told her he was sorry and that she had left him and she was wrong for going away. Deja' took that in, saying to herself, *Maybe I should understand. Perhaps if I did not go away he would not have cheated.*

Deja' was now visiting the betrayal space again, asking herself, *If I could be faithful while away, why not him?*

She forgave, and pressed forward with Rick and toward her dreams. Of course it happened again, and Deja' began to consider returning home from school. During this same time, she found out her mother Mia was incarcerated, and that was all she needed to confirm to herself that she needed to leave school and return home to save her relationship and also get to see her estranged mom.

Deja' and Mia rarely saw each other because she did not know where her mother was during these years. She only saw her periodically. Deja' returned home determined to finish college locally, save her relationship with Rick, and finally be able to have a relationship with Mia.

She started visiting her mom in jail and things were going well with Rick, or so it seemed. He did love her, however he wanted to be in a relationship and single at the same time.

Another infidelity took place, and Deja' was further devastated and planned to leave Rick. She left and moved in with her aunt Erica, who she was very close to.

Erica encouraged Deja' to continue to pursue her dreams. She supported her in college and would send her money periodically to help her make it through.

While Deja' was living with Erica, Rick continued to profess his love and offer apologies for his infidelities while promising it would never happen again. This was her first love, and a guy she wanted to spend her life with. She returned to live with him, and not long after he proposed.

It was a family affair, he did it in front of his whole family and she was shocked, excited and felt valued. In her mind, he really loved her and was truly sorry, and now she could have her very own *Little House On the Prairie*.

Her family supported it, too; Alice and Deja's sisters were so happy for her. She felt that things were turning out right in her life. She was with a man and family who loved her. Her godmother and sisters were happy that it was turning out well.

Deja's friends were excited for her also, but deep down inside she had doubts. When God is speaking, you may feel Him more than you hear Him.

Deja' wavered at times over whether they should get married. She wondered if Rick had really changed or was he just afraid of losing her.

Do you know that God gives you warnings? Well, think back over your life and see if you can locate the warnings: proceed with caution, or the stop, do not enter or other danger signs He threw up in your life.

I bet if you take a moment and scan your memory, there will be several, because God is always there cheering us on or giving us guidance. We just don't hear it or choose to ignore it.

There will be different things you will feel when this is happening, so listen for what you may have been feeling as you scan your life's experiences, and as I continue this now young woman's journey.

Deja' was confused and did not have anyone she could talk to who could really help her at the deep level she needed. She had overcome so many other things and was good at seeing the positive in everything, yet the little broken girl inside was still there and was now at a crossroads with no one to reach her.

Everyone along the way had only helped Deja' get through things, not heal things. She believed in God and always remembered her grandmother and how she saw life and said "God will work it out." This process helped Deja' get through many struggles, as it served as a source of light, but it also had implications of being a double-edged sword.

Some things are meant to be in your life but not meant to stay. Some things need to be cut off, but when your total thought is out of balance and you believe that God will work it out, in your immaturity you don't realize that Him working it out may mean you letting go of some things, not Him keeping you in your current situation.

As you will see further in the story, this view caused Deja' to hold on to things longer than she should have. She has tweaked this some in her adult life, but still holds allegiance to some parts of this view. Nonetheless in that moment this was her full and total view. We continue...

Deja' attended church and was saved because Alice would take the girls or send them every Sunday, and it was there that she found an anchor to hold on to at an early age, and now had someone she could reach out to at anytime, anywhere and anyplace. Deja' no longer needed to rely on someone making time to let her express her emotions or share her experiences, or worry about those emotions not being understood or downplayed. God became her primary source. He became not only someone to trust but someone to talk to and hear from for guidance. So in her mind she said, *God will show me what to do.*

She proceeded forward in the relationship out of love and trust that this man had changed, and continued the pursuit of her dreams. She enrolled in college locally and continued to study accounting.

Deja' and Rick got married. Mia was released from jail, and was Deja's maid of honor in the wedding. Her close girlfriends from high school and one of her sisters were bridesmaids, and her close friend since the age of 10 was her matron of honor. She was excited and happy.

Rick's mom Vi gave them a special gift, helping to pay for the wedding while they saved to put a down payment on a house. Deja' worked as a receptionist in Manhattan and attended night classes in college nearby.

While visiting her mom in jail, Deja' had become intrigued by the job of corrections officer and decided to take the test. One day, the New York City Department of Corrections sent a letter accepting her into the academy.

God was still involved.

She was a young woman now, but as a young girl, she had secretly struggled with fear of men. In her youth, if she was walking alone and a man was walking toward her on the same side of the street, she would cross the street or walk in the street to avoid walking past him. It was another secret Deja' covered up, as most would think she was crazy for feeling that way.

Not healing can have many consequences and impact your adult life. But once again, God uses everything, and although there is usually no formal healing when you grow up in the hood, your life experiences and the relationships you cultivate strengthen you and serve as a means to develop and heal you along the way.

There were many events that forced Deja' to face, deal with, and heal her scarred areas. This ultimately gave Deja' more power and the ability to handle life better as she got older. If she had never dealt with her fear of men, it could have caused her to be defeated.

She always felt that all a man wanted from her was sex, and that he was never interested in who she was as a person. She was always being told she had nice lips, hips or a sexy shape. She felt all she was to a man was whatever pleasure he could get from her.

Although he cheated, Rick made Deja' feel like she was worth more than sex—that she was smart, and had value. Although he subjected her to the very thing that had been a pain point for her for many years, taking away the value of her sexuality by cheating, Rick also fed her mentally and emotionally and was her biggest cheerleader. Deja' loved and honored him so much for that.

When I say God was still involved, He was. Deja' was getting what she needed to get to the next level.

Although she still had to suffer in other areas, God did not allow any of these disappointments to harm her. It was a balance of things that hurt and things that built.

In taking the corrections officer's job, Deja' sought stability, money, benefits and retirement, and it provided all of those things. Now she was married with a house and a mortgage at 21. Deja' felt she could do the job while still pursuing her dream of accounting, but corrections quickly put that to bed when she found out she would be on a rotating schedule, working various shifts. She opted to stay with corrections and put school on pause.

It was a good thing, because she ended up hating accounting and realized she would have been bored and living a life full of stress.

Taking the job also helped Deja' move past her fear of men in a huge way, and helped develop her leadership skills. She was working in jail, locked in with 100 men in a housing area. Not just men, but criminals.

God has a real good sense of humor. It's all about facing your fears and doing it anyway. That's the true definition of courage.

Rick supported Deja' taking the job and was very proud of her. He always encouraged and supported her dreams. Rick was her "road dog" through her struggles during these years, and helped encourage her along the way. They were happy.

There were still areas of concern in the marriage, because Rick was still hanging out, going clubbing, and had several single friends. Deja' would go out with him occasionally, and had a great time. She would also go out with her girlfriends and have a great time then, too. But she noticed this thing about him and women that still lingered.

Rick was her best friend but his interest in women would be their demise. See how the enemy is always seeking to destroy you with your issues? He knows the hand you were dealt and continues to try to play it for you in an attempt to cause you to lose the game of life. But know this: if you are at minimum seeking God, He will meet you where you are and help you navigate if you are humble enough to know that you are on a journey and living life in stages.

Always remain reflective and be honest with yourself as best you can; this will help you keep moving and be flexible.

Eventually Rick had another affair. Deja' started working the midnight shift and he started keeping company with a family friend who had been around for years. In fact, Rick and this woman had grown up together. She knew Deja' too, because she had been around the family for years.

The only question in Deja's mind was, how could he do this again? She was faithful, loyal and committed to Rick. Deja' was not ugly; in fact, men were always trying to ask her out, but she always said it was not worth losing her marriage for a temporary good feeling.

That thought alone was what always kept her faithful. It was not that Deja' did not find other men attractive in college, or in corrections, or even in the world, especially since Rick was the only man she had known sexually. She was curious, but committed.

It would never be worth it, even though Rick could have very well deserved it after the several affairs he'd had. Deja' could have used it as an excuse. But in her mind, she felt she was too smart for that and it was not in her character.

Deja' wanted to do what was right and not do anything to block her blessings, since God had brought her through so many things that could have destroyed her. Faithfulness, integrity, commitment and loyalty were important in all areas of Deja's life because she had experienced people and situations where they were not afforded to her. So when Deja' found out about this infidelity this time, she was at a crossroads again and it was time to make a decision. Deja' said to herself, *You can stay, knowing that this will continue, or you can leave and take the good that came from this and continue to build your life. If you stay and endure this again, you are setting yourself up to be destroyed.*

When the last affair happened, Deja' found herself on the verge of a breakdown, feeling unloved, unvalued, diminished as a woman and a wife. She felt betrayed in her own home—receiving the promise and commitment of fidelity after the I do's, only to find an I don't!

Deja' was shattered. She found herself in the bathroom on the floor, screaming, crying and kicking the tub, out of control because this betrayal was kicking up all the other betrayals, lies, abuses, pain and abandonment that she had put behind her, and now she felt out of control with emotion.

She knew Rick had to go to save her sanity, self-confidence, dignity and her dreams. No man or person would destroy all that God had brought her through. He had to go, period!

Always see yourself as the catalyst to make the necessary changes in your life, and never depend on someone else to do it for you. Even at your lowest point, stay grounded in your source; it will be your life raft.

At this time Deja' was, as mentioned previously, a corrections officer and carried a firearm. One evening, Rick's parents found out that Deja' was planning to leave him because of his many infidelities. They were shocked that Rick did these things.

Rick was ashamed, as he had the highest respect for his parents and wanted to ensure they always saw him in the most honorable light. He blamed Deja' for them finding out, but it was his own behavior with other women that brought the truth to light.

Well, Rick decided he was going to put some fear in Deja' because of his shame and embarrassment, so he unscrewed all the light bulbs in the house and stood at the front door, locking it from the inside to make the statement that she could not get out.

He had a screwdriver in his hand and very calmly was speaking in a somewhat gothic voice, asking, "Why did you do that? Why did you tell my parents all that stuff?"

Deja' answered, "It was your messiness that caused this and I only told the truth, but if you think you are going to hurt me in here tonight, please know that if you come toward me, I will blow your brains out and I am not playing."

Rick responded in a not-so-calm tone, saying, "You gonna shoot me? Maybe that is what's best. Go ahead, shoot me."

Deja' continued to say, "As long as you do not come toward me we are good!"

She was calm and resolute, and had no immediate fear of killing him or going to jail.

See how the enemy was continuing to try to destroy her? Let me be clear, Deja' had no clue about this spiritual warfare for her life that had been continuing from childhood. Yet God was determined to have her use her gift, of which I will share more later. Even writing this book is symbolic of it, although it is being written years later.

That night, Deja' slept on the couch—with one eye open, of course. The next morning, she spoke with Mia and David. During that conversation she told them what had happened the night before.

David, her stepdad, said, "You need to leave and get yourself out of that situation now!"

That day, Deja' packed all her clothes into her car, called Rick at work and simply said, "I'm leaving you."

He begged and said, "Wait, I am coming home, let's talk."

She hung up the phone, got in her car, and left.

I wish I could tell you it ended there, but it did not. Like I said, this is reality, and in reality, you do some things well and some not so well. The question is, are you willing to accept when you make the wrong decisions, and pick yourself up and try again knowing that you have already won? When you do not feel like it, are you are willing to navigate to get to your destiny no matter what hand you were dealt?

Play your hand and never lose yourself in any one mistake, hardship or circumstance, because as you will soon see, Deja' makes a wrong turn.

Chapter Six
A roller Coaster Ride of Confusion

Deja' left and went to Erica's house to pick up the pieces and start over again. This was the same aunt who had helped her in college and who she had roomed with for a few months.

They were close. Deja' could talk to her about things and they helped each other get through life. Deja' and Erica were girlfriends, besties.

Deja' stayed with her for a few months, and she talked on the phone with Rick as he tried to convince her to come back home, but she was not interested.

Deja knew Malcolm, an officer from work she had become friends with. Malcolm did not know anything about her personal life. They were cordial, and when they worked together they talked and were friendly.

After Deja' left her husband, she started to share some of what happened with Malcolm. They would talk a lot and Deja' found comfort in Malcolm. He made her feel special.

Malcolm gave her what she had been missing in her marriage. He worshiped the ground she walked on and let her and everyone else know it.

Deja' eventually became intimate with Malcolm. Meanwhile, Rick was still calling and wanting to talk. She finally engaged in a serious conversation with Rick, and they discussed all the hurt and issues in the marriage.

Deja' eventually started feeling torn between Malcolm and Rick. She still loved Rick, of course, and yet she was enjoying the love she was getting from Malcolm.

Bad move! Don't open another door until the first one is nailed shut. If you do, you are inviting confusion and buying a ticket to one of the worst roller coaster rides of your life.

Some of you reading this book can relate because you have been in this situation—either on purpose, getting back at someone, or by accident, looking for healing and restoration for yourself. The devil is a lie. You were broken, confused and in pain. You were not seeing clearly during this time and you picked based on what you needed at the moment.

So if you are reading this book and find yourself in a similar situation, please take these words seriously: Do not, I repeat *do not* say to yourself, my situation is different. Don't do it!

Give yourself time to get clear. Know, whether you agree or not, that the worst time to make a serious decision is when you are in a crisis. Most times it is the wrong decision.

Trust me even if you do not agree. Learn from others' journeys and mistakes, you will be glad you did later.

Deja' wished she had someone to speak in to her life during those times, to give her some course corrections. If she had, she would have avoided some pitfalls and been further along on her journey with fewer stops along the way to simply recover from life's blows.

These stops were necessary to maintain sanity and get clarity for the next move, but every time you have to stop you lose precious time. Now Deja' was at yet another crossroads; should she throw away all that she had built with Rick and take this journey with Malcolm, or should she reconcile with Rick?

As you are reading this, some of you are shouting at the top of your lungs, "Forget Rick and go with Malcolm." Then there are some of you who are saying, marriage is a commitment and sometimes things happen; if they can reconcile maybe they should, because they are invested.

Either choice might be right. The only caveat is, you must cut the husband off completely to start new with the new guy, or cut the new guy off completely and remain with the husband. There is no middle ground, so do your best to make a definitive decision if you find yourself in a similar situation.

Wisdom can take you far. Remember you are broken and not thinking straight; even if you think you are, you are not, and only time will reveal that to you. But do your best with what is at the core of you when making this choice. If you are a believer and praying on the matter, absolutely take the time to get answers.

I want to "jaywalk" for a moment over to the men who may be reading this book. Are you able to feel the pain that is sometimes caused by your hand? Do you see yourself in Rick?

Although this book is geared toward women, and is of course for all women, as a *brown* woman I can only share my culture. Our men have a huge opportunity, in that they can impact the face of our culture. It is you, men, who can enhance our culture by being, loving, loyal, faithful and integral to your women.

Have you had a woman who loved you and gave you chances to be right and do right, but you saw it as a weakness instead of a gift? Have you taken advantage of a woman who would do anything for you and left her broken? Are you still doing that?

I hope you see your current woman, or the women you have hurt in the past, as Deja' and it touches your heart to make a change at this very moment. If you are touched by this woman's story then *change!* Be the man she sees you can be; honor her and cherish her. She will be your backbone and you will be a part of changing the face of the *brown* family by impacting young men, by being an example and teaching our young women what a *real* man is.

Imagine the strength and power that will start from within the family unit. If you have ears, please hear!

The pain that is caused to an otherwise strong woman by lying, cheating, and abuse of her love is so damaging that it can change a woman's entire character. She can become a poor parent, not excel in her career, become promiscuous, lose hope in herself and give up on love entirely.

Do not be mistaken, we are strong as women and can and have overcome these betrayals by the men we love, and fight through it, as a lot of women have. But why should we have to? We preach unity as a people, yet we are not even unified as a family—instead of praising, we tear down. Instead of honoring, we undermine.

Deja' struggled in this area during that moment, but if she had known then what she knows now, her process for seeking answers would have been much stronger and she would not have chosen either Malcolm or Rick.

That probably shocks you—something you had not thought of, right? Here you are thinking you only have two choices.

Wisdom!

Well, at that moment Deja' was only thinking about the two options, too, and could not make a decision as to what was the best choice for her.

When you are broken you are confused and not clear. Mostly you are driven by your emotions and your pain. You may even start feeling sorry for yourself or the husband/man that hurt you, and start convincing yourself that perhaps this time he has changed.

What have you done in a similar situation? What did you learn?

Deja' did not go back right away; she continued to date Malcolm while she tried to sort things out in her head. One day, she decided to return home after much pressure from Rick. She told Malcolm she needed to go back home and see if it could work, and if it didn't, she would leave once and for all.

She returned home determined to leave Malcolm alone and pursue reconciliation with her husband. But instead of Rick feeling grateful and humbled by her return, he felt like it was her fault, and that what he did was not bad enough for her to leave him, and she should have returned home sooner. Not a good start, right?

Little things started to come up, like calls from other women claiming they were calling for innocent reasons but bold enough to ask for Rick and even ask for his work number too.

Rick made very popular mix CDs and people always wanted them, so calls about his CDs were common. These particular calls, however, were for more than CDs.

Rick's attitude was less than eager regarding fighting for the marriage. What do you think she did? Of course Malcolm was still waiting in the wings, periodically paging Deja' although she had asked him not to reach out to her, causing her to be confused. Deja' genuinely wanted to give her marriage a final try.

With all these things taking place and now causing her more confusion, making her question whether she had made the right decision, Deja' ended up meeting with Malcolm and yes, they were intimate on several occasions.

This was the roller coaster ride Deja' was not prepared for. She was now doing the thing she despised. She was stressed to the max, resenting Rick for not fighting and also resenting Malcolm who was encouraging her to live this double life.

If anyone had told Deja' she would be living that way, she would have dismissed it; this was so far out of character for her; it was like the Twilight Zone.

This went on briefly, but finally Deja' shut it down with Malcolm because she felt she was losing herself and everything she believed in. She was left depressed, lonely, confused and feeling like this was not the life she wanted.

What happens next will cause you to say, "See, she should have stayed with Malcolm."

One day Deja' received a call from one of Rick's close friends who said, "Hey, is Rick home?"

She replied "No," and continued with, "How are you? What are you up to?" Deja' found it odd he was calling—Rick had said he would be going out with this friend.

The friend said, "Nothing much, just working hard, but I saw Rick called me earlier and I missed his call because I am working the late shift today."

At that point Deja' was instantly upset, but continued the conversation because she did not want any confusion later when she confronted Rick about lying to her. She asked more questions and got confirmation that this friend was indeed at work, that day, at the time that he was calling, and was going to be there through the night.

When Rick came home in the middle of the night Deja' asked, "Is there something you need to tell me?"

Rick, as usual, tried to make her think she was crazy by saying, "Here we go, you're always trying to accuse me of something."

Deja' calmly asked, "Where were you?"

Rick proceeded to say, "I told you where I was," and continued on to claim he had been with the friend who had called.

She said, "Call him, let him tell me you were with him." Deja' never mentioned that he had called earlier.

So, being arrogant, Rick called the friend and started saying, "Hey man, sorry to bother you, but Deja' is over here bugging, not wanting to believe I was out with you."

She stood close to him and could hear the friend talking. She said, "Give me the phone."

Rick said, "Here, talk to her, man; she wants to talk to you."

He handed Deja' the phone and without hesitation she said, "Are you going to try to tell me you and him were together right now? Please let me hear you say that to me!"

The friend simply said, "Deja', please don't put me in the middle of this."

Deja' responded, "I thought so." She handed the phone back and went off!

Deja' began to tell Rick about the conversation with his friend a few hours earlier; she could hear the friend on the phone saying to Rick, "Come on, man, what are you doing?"

They finally hung up, and Rick knew he was busted so he confessed. Guess who he was with? The same woman he had the affair with that caused Deja' to leave months earlier. Really!

She felt stupid, and ashamed that she had even tried, coming back when she was already out. Now she had subjected herself to a greater pain, being outright taken for a fool.

This time was different, though; this time Deja' was totally calm and said, "You do not deserve me—I am done." She was, too!

The next day Deja' moved back to Erica's house and it was over! She had wasted nine months being miserable back with Rick, only to find out he was still seeing this woman and some others too. *How could I be so stupid*, she asked herself.

She had left with nothing; she walked away from her house and everything in it. Deja' only took the clothes she had and set out to start her life over again.

Chapter Seven
It's Not About You

Remember, you only have the hand you were dealt to work with. Can you feel stupid and still hold your head up high and know your worth? The experiences you are having are your coach and council, along with people who can speak into your life along the way. Choose them wisely, as everyone is not equipped to speak into your life. They can send you into further distress.

Most of Deja's friends came from similar broken homes and were trying to find their way also. They provided encouragement and a listening ear but were not in any position to deeply impact Deja'.

In a lot of cases, Deja' was the voice of advice for many of her friends. She, even in her marriage, and along her journey was considered wise in her own right. It is amazing how you can help other people and can't help yourself. Deja' had a friend who worked several years for a company and was tenured. She only had a few more years before retirement eligibility and was offered a supervisor's role. She was going to take it, but the exchange was that she would lose all her seniority.

Deja' shared with her that although this may be a great opportunity with a higher salary now, giving up security without a backup plan may be too high a price to pay in that no one knows what tomorrow may bring. If in a few years she took ill, she would not be able to retire, as that would no longer be an option. She could potentially be in a bad situation at her age, and looking down the road at putting in another 20 to 30 more years to be eligible to retire.

Deja' suggested she negotiate the offer to keep her seniority and if not she should weigh the odds before making a decision. The friend decided not to take the offer, as the potential impact of what she would be risking had not crossed her mind, and she realized it was not worth it. She was already working on getting a certification that would increase her salary, which is what she ultimately wanted, without her seniority being compromised, and she decided to fully pursue that path instead.

In another instance, Deja' was able to offer relationship advice to another friend. This friend's marriage was in turmoil with constant arguments and disagreements. Once the friend shared her view of the scenario, Deja' could clearly see, as she generally listens to put herself in both parties' position on the matter and not be biased because it's your friend telling the story.

It was evident that the two were in competition and did not value each person's role and power in the relationship. The husband was the breadwinner and therefore felt he should control all the money while letting (operative word "letting") her take care of the house and kids while she struggled through college in pursuit of her own career.

Deja' gave perspective, sharing that many women would be honored to have a man support them financially while they pursued their degree for a more solid career and instead of honoring him for that, her friend was minimizing it. He, on the other hand, was not valuing the work it took to study and raise children with homework, PTA, cooking/cleaning, studying and after school activities for the children.

Deja' advised sitting down and talking, without placing blame or competitive language like, let's see you take care of the house and kids while studying, or I can work too, you're not the boss because you make the money. Instead, she told her friend to thank him for maintaining the family while she pursued her degree. To tell him she was proud to be his wife, but also to share how some of the comments and financial decisions he made without including her made her feel. To tell him she would like to hear him say thank you for raising our kids to be strong, smart and well mannered. To ask him for more support in the evenings when she was studying. Give him special treats of gratitude during intimacy.

These are better routes to take than defensive confrontations and power struggles when you both love and are committed to going the distance together, so don't lose sight of the happiness you both want over lack of communication and understanding of one another's needs. Needless to say, she kept her friend from blowing up her marriage numerous times and is happy to say they are still married today, due not only to Deja's desire for happiness for her friend but also a grandmother who spoke wisdom to this friend and God's love for both of them.

Deja' has a knack for being able to listen to others' issues and being sensitive enough to perceive the root of a matter, not just the surface emotions. She is able to convey truths and perspectives that were not explored prior, that have helped correct or mend relationships.

There have also been times friends did not take Deja's advice, determining that she is too deep, only to return saying, "You were right." Deja', of course is not always right; all she tries to do is give the best advice that will benefit the person she is advising, while also weighing in on the person who is also involved and not able to tell their side because they are not present to do so.

All in all, it's the position of measuring the motivations of all involved by listening to what is not being said in the story. Deja' is not moved by the emotions, just the facts. Yes, empathy is required, because a person's emotions are their only ears at times, so you have to deliver what they are able to hear and then go deeper if they allow you. If they reject Deja's advice, she is also OK with that, and if they fall she simply tries to help them pick up the pieces without judgement.

Today, Deja' is able to draw from her own experiences to share with people the old phrase Feel, Felt, Found. "I know how you feel, I've felt that way before and this is what I found."

Side note: your gift will make room for you and it is usually for others not for you. Someone else has the gift that is for you. Deja' lived many of the lessons she has now been able to teach, allowing others to benefit from her journey.

Let me continue…

Chapter Eight
Temporary Insanity

It was not easy. Deja' was at another low place in her life. She felt humiliated, taken advantage of, used and totally devalued by this last experience with Rick. She noticed she was starting to become unemotional and reckless, no longer caring, only desiring to have fun and be free. She no longer trusted her judgement when it came to men, therefore why try?

Deja' rekindled the relationship with Malcolm, but things were different. She was bitter, and he was part of the whole situation, so while he talked marriage, that was the last thing she was interested in. Deja' had just got rid of shackles and although she loved Malcolm, she was not getting a new pair any time soon.

Malcolm resented her and could not understand Deja's brokenness and that the best route was for him to be a friend to her. Instead, Malcolm pressured her and told her to forget Rick, he was a creep and why are you still pining over that fool.

Deja' felt he did not understand and was being selfish. She could not be free to love him at that point in her life.

Eventually Deja' met someone else and told Malcolm she did not want to be in a committed relationship. He of course could not understand. Malcolm wanted her, and told her she should just get over Rick and live happily ever after with him. He absolutely could not understand why she wanted to date.

What Malcolm did not understand was where Deja' came from—that this betrayal was almost death to her, and now she was giving up on love and exchanging it for fun! Deja' decided she could not trust a man and to have a casual relationship was better.

She was willing to have that with Malcolm, but he was too deep and putting too much pressure on her. She had to distance herself. This new person Deja' became was embracing wanting to be guarded and not be affected by what a man could do to her.

Deja started dating the new guy and he was fun. He tried to convince her she was the love of his life but he was lying, she reasoned, and she didn't care, because she wasn't looking for love, only fun.

This is how self-deception and self-destruction can disguise itself and show up in your life. During that time, if you were a '70s baby and lived life a little as a woman, Mary J. Blige's *My Life* album was regularly played in your car. It was your anthem. For Deja', though, that season with this guy was about having fun, sex, partying, travel, drinking and that's it.

She didn't care if he loved her or not. Deja' did not love herself during this time in her life. Out at clubs on the weekend and sometimes on weekdays when she was off, she started drinking more regularly, although she could barely hold her liquor. She couldn't smoke weed because she was on the job but she sure wanted to.

Deja' wasn't crazy, not full-blown at least; she knew her job was her livelihood and would not do anything to risk getting fired. She did, however, start hanging out in places she would not go normally because of the type of crowd and potential element of danger present. Nonetheless, she had no concerns and it was fun.

She was having insane thoughts and fantasies of having a one-night stand. She had that chance when she ran into a puppy love she had when she was 13 during those summer visits to New Jersey and she took it. She also found herself dressing sexy, wearing outfits she would normally feel uncomfortable in. Ladies, if you are honest, you have been right here before! Nonetheless, Deja knew she was not in the right frame of mind and was wondering where all these thoughts and behaviors were coming from.

She had already had plenty of experience in her young life with being in the streets, at parties, being around drugs, prostitutes, drug dealers, and near misses of almost being raped or kidnapped.

During the early 90s in New York there was a van kidnapping young girls. The van would drive up next to young girls or ask a question and when the girl came close the sliding door would open and snatch them. Well, Deja had a friend, Tracy, who she grew up with from public school. Tracy and Deja were practically inseparable. They went to public school and junior high school together. They both had a lot of freedom and was into all kinds of unsupervised things at a young age. One day they were at Prospect Park, and it was getting dark, when they decided to head home. As they walked along the lonely street there was a van parked with no lights on. As they passed the van they heard a sound like the door was opening. They both was terrified and took off running. The vans lights came on but Deja was not able to run as fast as Tracy. Tracy picked up a pole or a stick and slowed down saying, give me your hand, and she pulled Deja to help her run faster.

She said, "their not going to take us without a fight". They never confirmed if it was truly the van kidnappers because it looked like the van was creeping slowly behind them as they periodically looked back. They stopped looking back, and before they knew it, the van was out of sight by the time they stopped to catch their breath. They never went to the park at night again unless they were with Tracy's brothers. They were like each others anchor. They went to bat for each other, lied for each other, and would fight anybody together and was not afraid. Tracy was courageous and fearless much more than Deja. They balanced each other out, thank goodness, because who knows they both may have come up missing. Deja was more cautious and rational so they played off of each others instincts. They did some crazy things together like, scrape food off their plate out the window and covered for each other not to get caught. They watched karate movies on Saturdays and acted out the moves on Tracy's brothers afterwards. They were pot heads and drank Cisco, only to have to drag each other into the shower drunk afterwards because one or the other got too drunk and threw up. They often snuck into the movie theater through the back door because they didn't have money to get in. They experienced a situation together, being in the wrong place late at night when they should have been home, that could have been traumatic for Deja. She was almost attacked by a grown man who was an acquaintance of Tracy's boyfriend. Tracy reacted immediately when Deja called out for help, even turning against her then boyfriend to defend Deja. They had some really fun times together but also had some really rough experiences together too. Growing up fast can be fun and dangerous at the same time. They are still in touch some 30yrs later and still talk about some of the fun and crazy times. They are grateful they are both here to talk and laugh about it now, because Deja' knows well that not everyone has that testimony.

It was common for her, when she was young, to be hanging out with older people who were associated with the street life. Deja' smoked weed, drank, skipped school (played hooky for those of you who are 40 and over), lied, and stole when she felt she needed to.

She was exposed to this lifestyle at a very early age, while most kids were home with parents probably watching cartoons. Deja' saw people smoke crack, shoot heroin and even helped cook, cut and bag it.

She had a double-barreled shotgun put to her head, and thought her life was ending that day. Well, she had many days she thought her life might end based on her experiences and the situations she found herself in. But God had plans for Deja'.

So if you think that you are alone as you go through life's challenges because you were dealt a crummy hand, know that the God who created you knows your hand and your destiny, and if you do not faint from life's ups and downs He will absolutely take you to your destiny. So trust him even when you can't feel Him, identify Him, hear or trace Him.

Deja's life could have gone in any number of directions. She had, as you can imagine, lots of freedom before being taken in by her godmother Alice, and even while with her, because she spent summers with Mia and at her grandmother's house, which also gave her freedom. She would be able to hang out with her older cousins and go to jams in the park and do what older people in their early twenties were doing.

What saved Deja' from sexual promiscuity were her early abuses. Her life experiences and the situations she put herself in caused others to think she was about that life. Your associations make you susceptible to being viewed a certain way and therefore become a target for abuse or being taken advantage of. The danger comes when they find out you are not a full participant and then try to force it on you. Although Deja was not a tease or a flirt she was a young attractive girl in an environment where you were expected to participate. Deja valued herself and did not feel she needed to give sex to get love or attention.

Those of you who have been molested, or who had multiple voluntary sex partners at an early age, and were used or taken advantage of, know that the feeling of being violated can mess your head up. Young girls who consent to sex early know about the soul ties and emotions that are felt when you are connected sexually to someone who hurts you.

Deja' still saw men as only wanting her for sex, and remembered the pain of being molested so vividly that she saw the two as synonymous. Therefore, sex was not of any interest to her during those times.

She believes God had His hand in that too. Allowing things that might hurt, but not things that would harm her during those very delicate years.

Deja' never dressed sexy except during that period of temporary insanity disguised as "fun"; even to this day she is very plain and simple in her everyday life. She will dress up depending on the occasion, but only rarely. She does not want the attention that dressing sexy brings.

When she worked in corrections, Deja' always wore a jacket, even in the summer when it was a million degrees behind those walls, because she did have a nice shape and she did not want the inmates to see any more than what they were already imagining.

Your experiences stay with you and you can reach back and get them anytime. So when Deja' was deciding she no longer wanted love, and was entertaining this random guy just for fun, she was able to pick that street lifestyle and persona back up very easily, and now it did include sex. All in the name of fun, but the truth was she was numbing and self-medicating to try to get past this last low point of being deceived yet again by Rick.

Deja' was indeed enjoying it that way until she woke up next to him one day and thought, *What are you doing?*

God will tap you on the shoulder even in your mess and say, *Daughter, this is not the life I have created for you. You have come too far to devalue yourself the way you are right now. Your future is waiting for you and it is a life you will be proud of.*

The Devil will seek to have you repeat your past, duplicate or have you emulate the people or situations from your past that almost destroyed you. Pain can make you unconscious even while you appear to be walking around wide awake.

Once you are jarred awake, you go through shame and feel sorry for yourself and think you are worthless. But what the Devil means for evil, God uses for good. God makes you feel convicted not condemned, corrected not counted out.

Take that as a nugget so you will from this day forward know the difference, and the source of what you are feeling, and act accordingly. If what you are feeling is making you feel condemned and worthless, you know it is not coming from God and need to dismiss it immediately, because if you do not you will be in grave danger. You will find yourself doing even more destructive things to yourself and others.

Whereas if you feel conviction and correction—that strong desire urging you to do better—it will prompt you to improve, change and grow. That's God! But as we know, life is a journey, healing is a process and most of the time you are not standing still while your life unfolds.

So Deja' decided she wanted to settle down, and Malcolm was still in the picture, but he did not feel exactly the same anymore, unknown to her and perhaps even to himself. Deja' also did not ever really get a chance to fully see him as a life partner before.

They began seeing each other again, since he seemed to still really love her and worship the ground she walked on. They both agreed they wanted to have a serious relationship with each other. But remember, when you are broken, you pick based on what you need at the moment. Now that she was back thinking about a relationship and moving forward, being productive and deepening her spiritual life, she realized that there were crucial things that they did not have in common.

The problem was that Deja' had now fallen in love with Malcolm. Through all her mess, she still believed in God, which is what I believe pulled her through her life to that point. These things didn't matter when she was reckless, but now that she was in love, they did. The opposite of what normally happens when you love someone. But Deja' always believes that what is closest to you has the most influence over you, good or bad. She may not have always been faithful to God but she was sure afraid of something or someone separating her from Him right under her nose.

Malcolm did not believe in God. She had known that before, but it mattered now as she was trying to find herself again and was now looking at him and their future together in a more serious light. Over the years, Malcom attended church with Deja' and she always hoped he would one day believe, but during conversation it was always clear that although he enjoyed the service and the message at church he felt it was like going to listen to a motivational speaker, not that God had anything to do with it. This always made Deja' nervous but she tried to stay optimistic that one day he would change, he just had not arrived at that reality yet.

Malcolm resented her for this, especially after how she had treated him. Once again I will repeat, and also give context to: do not open a new door until the other is nailed shut.

Malcolm saw Deja's mess while it unfolded. He did not see God in her, and thought she abused his love, even if it wasn't deliberate.

Perhaps Malcolm might have been saved if she was not being self-destructive. Deja' did not blame herself for that, though, because only God can call you. Nonetheless, we also have to take responsibility for being light, and we don't get a pass just because we are going through something.

Deja' always remembered that and made a vow going forward that no matter what crisis she was going through to always be a godly example as best she could, because it's not about you. God uses you to be a blessing to others even when you feel like putting your Christianity in the sock drawer for a few days, weeks, months, a year or even years. You do not have that luxury.

Please be clear, Deja' is not a perfect Christian and never has been, so this book is not a Bible-toting woman telling a story; this is a real woman like many of you reading this, who loves God but at the same time was and can still be a hot mess. Don't judge her or yourself.

God is your judge, not man. There are many Christians who outwardly proclaim God yet privately live like heathens and have the nerve to judge others. If we were perfect we would not need grace, forgiveness or correction, let alone salvation.

So know that Deja' is not by any means perfect, but she found and had at an early age a source of power, although it was not fully developed and often went untapped. Still, it was her anchor and her guide.

As you can see, Deja' fornicates, makes poor choices and does not always seek God before making decisions. She is definitely a work in progress. Do not let anyone ever tell you that because you are not a perfect Christian that you are not a Christian, because there are countless stories in the Bible of people who lied, cheated, even killed, and yet loved the Lord. There is even a story of a man who committed adultery, had a baby with this woman and had her husband killed to cover it up. Yet God said this was a man after His own heart.

But let me make clear, this does not give you a pass to live any old way, God does expect you to live a certain way and follow certain principles. That is why He gives you grace and the opportunity to change and follow Him. Please strive to be the person God wants you to be and try to live the way God wants you to live by seeking Him.

You may not have arrived yet, but I would be remiss not to tell you the truth—that when you are not living by godly principles, there are consequences. Therefore let me not give you a false impression: When you are doing things that are not in line with God's plan for your life, you will learn, and the lesson is painful at times, but He loves us enough to not leave us the same.

Nevertheless, if we could be perfected by our own strength we would not need Jesus. With that said, I repeat it does not give you a pass. God knows your heart and if you are willingly living terrible and resting on grace, God knows, so don't play with that.

Be your best, do your best and let God do the perfecting with you being authentic, genuine and fighting to be and live right all the way. That is grace because He does for you what you are not able to do for yourself. He builds the bridge for you to cross into greatness.

Chapter Nine
Repeating the Past While Struggling to Get the Lesson

Deja' continued to date Malcolm, traveling a winding road of differences in values and life views. He started to display behaviors that she was familiar with. Malcolm would look in lust at other women, and flirt with other women, including her friends. Sadly, some of her friends flirted back, but she did not say anything. She simply said to herself, *how could they do this?*, knowing they would have a fit if she did those things to them.

Malcolm and Deja' went on dating for several years. Although his behavior never revealed actual cheating, it brought Deja' pain nonetheless.

Deja' felt Malcolm was capable of cheating, and possibly just had not gotten caught yet. They would argue and break up and then get back together.

They did this several times over the years. More and more, Deja' wanted to remarry, and felt that because of the way the relationship had begun, with all the craziness, it might never work.

Malcolm continued to profess his love to her, as did she to him, so they continued. Deja' continued because she felt she could right the wrong she had done to him in the past, and if he really did love her and forgave her it would work.

As she was on her recovery path and had started attending church regularly again, working to rebuild herself, she decided she wanted to be abstinent, but Malcolm was opposed. She had tried this unsuccessfully several times; Malcolm would act like it was a crime for her to want to do this after they had already been having sex.

People, places and things—you have a pull to live right, but people in your circle can make it challenging at times. It is hard to make necessary changes when you are not surrounded by people who nurture that change.

What does your circle consist of? Deja' had a mix of people who saw her potential and encouraged her, and people who wanted her to remain the same because it was their comfort zone.

It was a tug-of-war of sorts. As she tried to get her life right, she struggled because they were not on the same page with her and couldn't understand why she was having this inner turmoil. But I remind you, once you belong to God, He will cause you to battle with right and wrong, pushing you constantly to choose good.

I hope some of you reading this book can relate to this inner battle and know now, if you did not know already, that this constant tug-of-war is because the hand you were dealt was a losing hand. You may have some jokers in it, along with a hand full of hearts and clubs, and have no clue how to play that hand without cutting your partner or getting stuck (that's an analogy for those of you who know how to play spades).

Your hand is dealt, you now have to figure out how to play it and maximize on your books. It's not always easy, you have to play a few hands and sometimes switch partners (friends, family, mates, jobs, locations, etc.) to get the right fit. At times you play off your partner's hand, or connect with a master player to teach you how to navigate the game. Either way, your hand is your hand, and no one can play it but you.

One day, Deja' decided she was going to put her foot down. Since they had been talking about marriage, she was going to be abstinent for real. She discussed this with Malcolm, only to have him say he was not doing it, and if she would not have sex with him he would find someone else who would.

She was devastated. It took Deja' back in her mind to the times in her life where she had felt that all a man wanted from her was sex. Hearing these words come out of Malcolm's mouth crushed her.

Deja' told him if he felt that way then yes, he should go find someone else. They broke up, and she was sad, but felt confident that she had made the right decision because they were not going in the same direction in life.

A few months later Deja' found out he was having a baby; he had indeed gone and found someone else. Deja' was hurt but still felt she had made the right decision.

Malcolm, on the other hand, spent several years dealing with the well-known term "baby mama drama." It caused him to be homeless for a time, stressed to the max and feeling like his whole life had been turned upside down.

Malcolm was remorseful, saying he wished he had chosen to be abstinent, because the day when he said those words to Deja', his life spiraled out of control.

Malcolm has a beautiful, intelligent daughter who he loves dearly and has made many sacrifices for, and would do it all again if he had to. There is a blessing even in our missteps, but the relationship between Malcolm and Deja' was never the same. At one point, they tried to rekindle their relationship, but he was even more different.

Deja' was very accepting of his child, for she had not asked to be here; she was innocent and deserved love like any other child. Malcolm was so caught up that once again he took Deja' through changes where she felt she was not a priority.

The baby's mama had the same grip on Malcom that Rick once had on Deja' several years before, yet Malcolm continued to insist the situations were different. They went through some rough times indeed. Malcolm was reckless, inconsistent, dishonest and all these behaviors landed Deja' in a love triangle of sorts.

Choices can sometimes take you down a rabbit hole. Each choice you make sends your life in a different direction. But the question is, how far down that road do you go before you realize you have made a wrong turn? Do you keep going, thinking it's a circle or feeling too ashamed to turn back? Or do you say to yourself, *I am lost, let me turn back and get back to where I knew where I was and make a right turn this time?*

It is all in how you see yourself and your mistakes. Be willing to turn back and get back on the right path—your life depends on it.

You may be asking yourself what is wrong with Deja'. Why did she stay in apparent bad relationships? Great question!

You may already recognize the problem, and may even be saying, that is me, or I have done that same thing so many times. Or you may be saying, no way—I would have been gone a long time ago.

Something worth noting for those of you who do self-reflections: Abandoned, love-starved, abused children grow up to be adults that pick people who betray, abandon, and abuse them, and who are emotionally unavailable, because that is what they are used to even subconsciously.

I will also say, don't judge Deja'—see her journey and identify yours. Your strengths may be her weaknesses and her strengths may be your weakness.

One thing Deja' noticed was that she had many friends, including some even to this day, who would say, "Girl, I would have never dealt with that. You crazy!" or, I would have done this or that. You may have friends like that too.

Learn how to filter that information out, because you will find that these are the same people you watch in similar situations do the same kinds of things, or do the same kinds of things in their particular areas of weakness. They will even make the same kinds of choices in their own situations.

For those reading this I am sure you too have struggled in your areas of weakness. So do not judge, or say what you would do, if you have not lived it or if in your own life situations you make or have made similar choices and errors.

That is why it is important to encourage, have compassion and tell the truth in a spirit of love, not criticism. Be your sister's keeper. Lift her up, do not tear her down, for you too have been down or will be in the future.

What will you do when your tough decision comes? Women who were dealt a hand of abandonment and betrayal, who have been used and hurt, desire healthy relationships but attract people who are not healthy. They may even sabotage their relationships to a degree, because they subconsciously expect things to go wrong at some point.

In the case of Deja', she was learning herself and trying to stop having to take the same courses over and over again in order to get the lesson.

She maintained a close relationship with Rick because their families were close, and although he had done the things he did to hurt Deja', he had also been there for her in ways that no one else had, including her family. Perhaps they were only meant to be best friends, not mates, because Deja' would have given her right arm for Rick and vice versa.

Rick was very consistent with his commitment to making sure Deja' was good, and if she needed him for anything he was right there, no strings attached. Rick was—and is, believe it or not—one of her best friends to this day. Deja' can count on him to have her back in the rough times and be her cheerleader in the good times.

Rick had serious issues with women but that aside, he was a true and dear friend to her. So much so that they tried again to rekindle after they divorced, and what raised its ugly head was almost laughable. Exactly!

It was something to do with a woman and him being less than honest. Well, that truly was the grand finale—she was completely and unequivocally done at that point, and it has been many years now and they simply love each other as family and are the best of friends.

A similar thing happened with Malcolm. Deja' remained friends with him over the years as well, and a few years after the drama decided to give it another try too.

They discussed marriage again. By this time she was living in North Carolina.

A note of wisdom: Stop bringing old stuff into your new place. When you move, do you bring all your stuff from one house to the next, or do you leave some and throw some away? You leave some and throw some away! If not, you end up cluttering the new place and not having room for anything new, and eventually end up throwing it out later anyway. Another class and another lesson!

Chapter Ten
What Kind of Love is This!

When Deja tried with Malcolm again, she was considering moving back to New York after she was in a new place that she loved, in her current job as a bank manager, and had at that time purchased and was renting two investment properties. What was she thinking?

Deja' was perplexed by the thought of moving. She wondered who would take care of the properties, how she could start over with a new job and deal with the stress of living in New York again.

Deja' prayed about it endlessly, and one day during her time of prayer while ranting to God about what she was going to do with the houses and how she was going to give up her nice place and the comfort of living in North Carolina, God responded, and it was almost as though He was right there in the room speaking audibly.

She heard Him say, "You're asking the wrong question."

Deja' immediately stopped and said, "What, what is the question?"

Almost immediately the response was, "The question is, is Malcolm your husband?"

Deja' instantly had a different perspective. She thought, *Right!*

What God was saying was, if he is your husband, the man you are supposed to be with, none of what you are asking matters because you will be gaining more than you would be giving up. However, if he is not your husband, then you are taking a huge step backwards and walking away from the path to your destiny.

She was amazed and in awe. Deja' did not make any decision at that point; she just meditated on that question from that day forward.

Fate would have it that a family member would go into the hospital a short time later, and Deja' needed to go to New York to care for them. Deja' stayed with Malcolm that week she was there, and everything, I mean everything that God had revealed to her became crystal clear.

She returned home after that trip and knew beyond a shadow of a doubt what God meant when He had asked, is he your husband? Malcolm was not ready to be married; he was not ready to be the man Deja' needed him to be. There was not an issue of another woman, it was simply the realization that he was not "husband ready" for what Deja' knew she wanted and needed from the man she would marry.

It was finished. They, too, would remain friends with no more question of a possible reconciliation. They remain friends to this day.

That is another question to ask. Why does Deja' remain friends with people who hurt her, and keep ex-boyfriends and ex-husbands as friends? I will say this first.

Deja' has asked at times, *God, with all the stuff and mistakes I have made, why do you keep pulling me out of harm's way? Why didn't you let either of these bad relationships destroy me?*

The simple answer was, God loved her and saw that she was foolish, forgiving and continued to hope for the positive, and treated people, including each of these men, as if they had never hurt her.

I will revisit the gift story for you. Deja' has been told many times that she is a best friend, she is loyal to a fault and no matter what happens, can be counted on to have others' best interest at heart. She has been told that when she is down for you she is down for you regardless, even if you have hurt her.

Your gift is in you even when you do not want it, because it is not for you, it is for other people. It is a double-edged sword, because helping others comes naturally for Deja' and even when she is hurt by people, she still almost automatically has an image of what's good about them that prevents her from full-blown anger and retaliation.

Sometimes she wants to be angry, yet is unable to because all that flashes through her head is the good she sees in them, and it makes her angry at herself for not being able to hate them. She will, however, cut you off for crossing her, yet still will not repay you for your evilness.

She is grateful that she has a huge heart but honestly speaking, sometimes she would like to at least desire to make them pay. Instead she ends up feeling sorry for them. This does not apply only to men, but people in general. However, regarding these two men and her handling of them, both will say emphatically that they are the men they are today because of Deja'.

She loved them unconditionally when they were not worthy and allowed them to remain in her life after they tried, intentionally or not, to destroy hers. Both Rick and Malcolm assert that many of their successes are due to Deja' constantly believing in them and bringing out the best in them. They say to this day that there is nothing they would not do for Deja', and if she would have either of them back they would be the best husband she could ever imagine. Deja', however, will assert that they indeed may be genuine in their intent to be the best husbands, but can only have confidence in what she has experienced with these men.

They have been great friends to her over the years but were very poor lovers. Several years have passed but Deja' used to wonder why she continued to give them numerous chances over long stretches of time.

After much thought she realized that although she was very forgiving and did love them both, as that was in fact part of it, there was something deeper. Their commitment to her during very significant times in her life was the true key to her being loyal in spite of them.

Unknown to them, there were situations where they did something of significant value for Deja' that created a bond greater than the hurt they caused. In Deja's opinion there is a difference between motivation to hurt and defects of character. In simple terms: don't cross her!

You may have human flaws that caused you to disregard a person's feelings because of your selfishness, and that can be forgiven. However, ill intent, maliciousness or a premeditated agenda to cause harm gets you the forgiveness of heaven but here on earth, she is done with you! Deja' is no stranger to pain, yet holds loyalty to those who are there for her during times she deems crucial.

Deja' was there during their struggles in life, either with work, a child, or crazy relationships with different women, friendship issues or simply just needing a friend at times. Deja' never wavered and was always there as a friend to them. She gave them heartfelt and genuine advice, encouragement and insight that helped them on their life's journey.

Both of them know they can never have another chance at love with Deja', but they fear that her kindness, and the level of love and understanding that she gives once she loves someone, will cause her to be hurt by another man who does not see her value and uniqueness.

Imagine, after 30 years with the man who was her husband and 20-plus years with the man she met after her husband as friends, after all the drama, to have impacted their lives so deeply that they would make statements like, "I am me because of you, and you were my greatest failure." That is because it was not Deja', it was her gift.

That same gift allowed her, after all the abandonment and neglect she suffered from her mom, to now have a relationship closer than that of most mothers and daughters who lived healthy lives together. The ability to forgive and love people who hurt you as if it never happened, and be a blessing in their lives, can be described in no other way than as a gift.

It was placed in her at birth to give to the world, whether the world was ready to embrace it at the time or not, because your gift is not for you, it is for others. Someone else has your gift, and Deja' over the course of her life has been given many gifts from others.

What's your gift?

The journey continues…

Deja' loves her job, but her dream is freedom—financial freedom and the freedom to make an impact on other women's lives by teaching them how to overcome the hand they were dealt. She wants to purchase more investment properties as well, and be free to live life without a job.

Deja' continues to be encouraged by many who confirm her gift is alive and thriving. She has been told many times that she should have been a counselor, a minister, or a mom, because she is nurturing, and so many have called on her for advice or to get insight into the issues that they face.

What they say is, "I know you will tell me the truth and will not judge me. I know you have other people's best interests at heart, and put yourself in their shoes to give them the best advice you can." There are many people who have said, "If something happens to me, I want you to raise my children," or even call her when they meet with a crisis—sometimes before they call their husbands.

They will also tell you Deja' is stubborn and can rub you the wrong way. She can be very direct and strong in her delivery at times, and can bruise you with her forwardness and strength.

Sometimes leaders leave a lot of dead bodies in their wake, so you really have to balance a good dose of love with the strength you possess. People do not care about how much you know until they know how much you care.

Deja' has the long lasting relationships that she does because anyone who knows her knows that she is a true friend and is loyal, honest, dependable, and can be counted on. If you find yourself in a situation, you know you can call Deja' anytime, day or night, and she will not be too busy for you. You can cry and be weak and vulnerable and she will not judge you, but will find a way to help you get back up and keep on moving.

Deja' will sacrifice herself for you even when you do not deserve it. That is why she has a very small, close-knit group of people in her life who she has known since childhood, but not a large group of casual acquaintances.

Deja' does not do acquaintance; you are either a friend or not, period. She gives too much of herself to waste it on acquaintances.

Deja' likes to spend time alone, and does not need a partner to go to the movies, travel, out to dinner or to just hang out. Yes, she enjoys doing these things with others at times, but can also enjoy doing them alone.

Deja' is comfortable in her own skin and loves herself even when others do not. It's OK for her.

Yes, she has her share of disappointments when she goes all out for others and realizes they do not appreciate her, but she knows that her blessings are stored up and she will lack for nothing.

Deja' chooses to continue to give of herself and have the best interests of anyone in and out of her circle at heart. Her life has brought her many accomplishments and lots of things that she is proud of.

The little abandoned girl who had nothing and who was counted out by many is now someone who loves herself and does not need validation from anyone except God. She is someone who has excelled in her career, became an entrepreneur, and is inspirational and admired by many.

God says, *I know the thoughts I have for you are to make you prosper and not harm you, and to give you a hope and a future.* So as Deja' has had great accomplishments on her journey, her struggle over the years has continued to be men. They love her sensitivity, deep affection, and wisdom, while at the same time hating her strength and confidence.

The same things that make them love Deja' are the reasons they hate her or want to cut her down to size; it is a double-edged sword. Either they are intimidated by her accomplishments and strong personality or the fact that Deja' does not need what the average woman needs.

She does not need a man to take care of her, or pay her bills, or help her make decisions. She needs a friend, a man who can love her passionately, who is loyal, honest, who has integrity and dreams of his own. A man with a "go-get-it" attitude without excuses, and who is compassionate, communicative, vulnerable at times and not intimidated by her status. Someone who can understand her journey of pain and how it is a big part of who she is today. A strong man, who does not have to exert his strength over her to put her in her place, but will highlight her strengths because he is strong in his own right. A man who looks at her as his queen and can accept her past and her brokenness while correcting her, bringing out the best in her, even pointing out her flaws and faults in love, while raising her to new heights. Someone Deja' can share the deep matters of the heart with, and make him her king. Not having to withhold love to prevent him from seeing her as weak, green or gullible because she is so predictable, transparent and willing to take you at your word. That should be an honor for a man, not a pass to live like a tyrant and drag her heart in the wake of his destruction.

Deja' has seen enough and lived enough that "green" would not be the right word to describe her—if she measured and treated people based on her life experiences, she herself would be the tyrant wrecking everything in her path. Deja' has learned enough to be able to manipulate, take advantage of or use others, but she knows that if she used her gift for evil, there would be a hefty price to pay, so she reminds herself always to stay humble, kind and sensitive to others.

She sees things and you will not know she sees them, because she pays attention to details and holds them in her brain. She becomes sad when she knows someone is lying to her or trying to deceive her, or she knows that she has been betrayed by someone, yet she gives them the benefit of the doubt, in the hope that they will see her value and change. And if they do not, she now knows internally she has to prepare herself for the fallout.

Deja', however, does try to warn the person that doing the right thing or being honest is best, without saying, *I know what you have done, said or are doing thinking I have no clue.* Deja' would really like to have someone change on their own, not because she put them on blast.

Now, she can and has put people on blast at times to let them know, *Please don't take my kindness for weakness, I stay loving and committed to you not because I see you as a saint, but because I choose to see the best in you, not the worst, and want to bring out your best and not condemn you because of your mess.* So in the area of men, the challenge continues.

Deja' dates, but has now vowed not to give ten-plus years to a situation that is destined for disaster. She places a set of rules on her relationships, and is willing to walk away once she discovers this is not a love connection with a future.

Deja' is not as judgmental regarding a man's inherent flaws, if they arise out of being a black man in a world that is already against him, and the things he suffered and became because of it. But she does look for his control over the things that self-development, self-discipline, self-love and love for others should manifest.

Everyone who strives to be better must work on themselves, respect themselves and others, not be haters but motivators, game-changers, and know how to love, honor, and respect a woman. These are things that can be learned, and are part of character.

Your character is who you are in private and public. The road to failure is paved with good intentions, so don't intend to be good, just be good.

So this lesson that she learned over the years has served her pretty well. Deja' dated a few people, but let it go within a reasonable period of time when she saw they did not have her best interests at heart.

This can be a bit tricky, because people put their best foot forward in the beginning, but very quickly start to show signs of poor character and you must be sensitive to this above your physical attraction and, in her particular case, the desire to help a person be better.

Chapter Eleven
When the Enemy Plays Dress-Up

Deja' has learned that help is reserved not only for those that need it but those who receive it. So when you see certain things manifested, make the decision and make it fast. Move on.

She did this for a few years, and felt very proud of herself. However, a man came in to Deja's life, who she initially was not attracted to—she was happy being single, and had been for some time when she met Marcus. She was chasing her dream and was not looking at all.

Marcus came along and was around Deja' in a work setting, so she still was not thinking anything of this man. For a couple of months they were in a work setting together, and Marcus started making subtle comments reflecting an interest in her. Deja' was a bit surprised, as she had no idea he had even been sizing her up.

This continued for a period of time, until a situation came up that required Deja' to call Marcus. That evening, he called her and left a message. Deja' texted back a response as she did not see the call as anything relating to her, but only regarding the work situation she had called him about earlier in the day.

They continued to text back and forth that evening, and Marcus revealed that he had been attracted to her since they met, and would like to get to know her. Deja' was a bit nervous, as she was not looking or thinking about dating anyone at the time and wondered if she should give it a chance.

She continued to text, and started talking to Marcus and even went out with him a few times. Deja' loved his smile and he appeared to be sensitive, have a dream and ambitions in life. She was intrigued. Marcus was funny, street smart, believed in God and attended church.

Note, just because you claim to believe and attend church does not mean you have a godly character. This is an important point, so please do not take what I just said lightly.

Nonetheless, Deja' started dating Marcus, and over the weeks and months she noticed something different than she had in any previous relationship. She could not get a read on Marcus.

They were spending a lot of time together, but Deja' continued to have a nagging feeling inside saying, *You do not know him. This relationship is surface level.*

Deja' could not figure it out, and continued to try to go deeper attempting to get to know Marcus. Yes, he shared life experiences he had, and they talked about childhood and family, but something kept ringing inside her saying, *You are missing something, you do not know him still and there is a block up that is invisible.*

Deja' would constantly tell her friends that she liked Marcus and had fun with him and the relationship was moving along but there was something she couldn't figure out. He was mysterious, and as she tried to get closer to him he evaded her.

There would be last minute things that would come up with friends, or having to travel for a family emergency.

These things threw up red flags, but Deja' did not want to let her past trust issues dictate her life so she said, let me let things unfold and not jump to conclusions.

Marcus did share that he had been married before, and had children who he loved and talked about often. Marcus loved his mother, and always talked about wanting her to be proud of him. He showed his sensitive side on many occasions and professed honesty, loyalty, faithfulness and that one should trust until given a reason not to trust.

Deja', on the other hand, felt trust was earned, not given. She tried to think of it as just a difference of opinion, but periodically she would catch him in a lie without saying anything. She was starting to say, OK, it's time to pay closer attention.

But Marcus was still capable of being sweet, loving, caring, and attentive while also being distant, evasive, and quick on his feet to wiggle out of things.

Deja' gave him the benefit of the doubt, but was putting together pieces of a puzzle without knowing what the end picture was going to be. She could tell that there was something deeper about this man that she did not know.

Her friends could not decide what it was either. They kicked around "Is he married?", but he talked freely about his ex-wife and offered Deja' keys to his place and wanted her to stay over often, she explained. Deja' could speak to Marcus on the phone anytime, day or night, and he spent the night often. So no, she concluded, he was not married or involved with someone else.

Did I mention that he liked to travel? Every other month or so, Marcus would travel to New Jersey or New York to handle family issues. Deja' could speak to him on the phone then, and he sent pictures of himself with the family also. So while she had questions, there was no definite deception about what Marcus was doing during his visits out of town.

Deja' asked Marcus outright, "Do you have a baby or a family in New York?" He immediately said no. She had no proof, so she just put it in the back of her brain and continued on.

When they would get in to serious conversations Marcus would say things like, "You are too deep." Yet Deja' was saying, "You are too surface level."

By this time they were intimate and were enjoying each other and spending time together. Marcus wanted to come over every night. Deja' had to get used to this, because she was used to being single and living alone, so she had to adjust, especially since she had begun to really care about Marcus.

Marcus would give her nice thoughtful cards and bring flowers to her job. He would rub her feet, cook for her, serve her, and she was flattered and looked forward to seeing and talking to him daily. In the midst of all of this, though, there was still questionable behavior like looking at other women—not just a glance, but looking almost with the thought of, *I wonder what that would be like?*

Deja' called Marcus on it, and he tried to make her feel that she was bugging and had insecurity issues. Then Marcus admitted he did like to look at other women, but not with the intention of disrespecting her, and he promised he would stop doing it. That of course didn't happen. I understand that as a man when you see an attractive woman you will look because you are human. However, as a woman, and your woman, I should not see you starring or consistently looking and checking another woman out. It is disrespectful and makes a statement to the other woman regarding me. As women we see when a man is checking us out, and if he is with his woman when he is doing it, we automatically either feel sorry for her, or think he is not that in to her. I am speaking from experience being a woman who is disgusted when a man who is with his lady, and is sending me signals behind her back or over her shoulder.

Marcus also liked to go to events and clubs if someone was throwing a party. He always had a friend who was throwing a party, and usually there were strippers there, or they would go to strip clubs for someone's birthday. Deja' did not agree with that, because what man in his forties still enjoys going to strip clubs, if he is not going to look at the women?

Again, not a 20- or 30-year-old; a 40-plus-year-old. Now the road was getting a bit winding, because they were starting to have arguments about Marcus's behavior and mysteriousness, and he was very good at trying to flip it around on her.

Imagine two psychology majors having an argument. It was special. But Marcus would argue his point and Deja' would argue hers.

Deja' was very transparent about her past and her relationships with the men in her life. Marcus, however, tried to take it and use it as a weapon against her and try to make her weak by depicting these men as people who used her and were still using her, and then accusing her of still possibly sleeping with them.

It was all smoke and mirrors; inside, Deja' said, *Lord really, why do I attract men who want to abuse me and take my kindness for weakness?*

Marcus's behaviors were questionable on several fronts: travel, looking at other women, still having a close relationship with his ex-wife, which was normal because they had children together so that was not a problem for Deja'. However, he complained about her friendships with Rick and Malcolm, while having female friends and showing no concern about telling a strange woman she was beautiful in front of Deja's face and adding, "Let me introduce you to my son because you're too young for me".

Marcus meanwhile, would question Deja' about a bank customer, who happened to own a restaurant that she periodically ate at, bringing her lunch. Marcus checked her phone while she was in the shower once, and read a letter she had typed about him that was saved in a folder on her computer that was labeled My Feelings. While Marcus used her computer for his homework, he read that letter without Deja's permission, and brought it up to her days later.

Marcus denied checking her phone, but she knew that he had, because she knew where she had left it when she went into the shower, and it was positioned differently when she came out.

Deja' did not question it—she let it go until one day Marcus claimed she sent him a text by mistake. When he told her what the text said, and the name it was sent to, Deja' knew for sure that he had checked her phone.

Marcus had seen a similar name to Malcolm's in her phone, and a text that sounded like a date to visit him, and ran with it. But the text was to her brother in-law about coming to visit her father-in-law, who had a terminal illness.

As they talked about it, Deja' asked Marcus to forward the text to her and he said he had deleted it. OK! So the lie was solidified; at that point, there was no sense in discussing it further. Marcus had apparently made up his mind he would be taking this lie to his grave.

Deja' wondered, though, why he was always claiming she was insecure and that her past relationships had messed her up when Marcus was checking her phone, and reading letters on her computer, and questioning her friendships with Rick and Malcolm.

Meanwhile, Marcus was out at the strip club, looking at other women, and having female friends who, when they called him, he answered the phone "Hey, babe," right in front of Deja' and held conversations that, yes, seemed to be platonic, but still—it was like he did not realize his behavior was inappropriate. Yet he defended himself at every turn.

Chapter Twelve
It All Comes Out In the Wash

Marcus wanted Deja' to completely cut off her male friendships out of one side of his mouth, but from the other side would say, "I am not saying you can't talk to your friends, just respect our relationship." But Deja' respected herself first and foremost and would not allow anyone, even the men in her past, to disrespect Marcus.

One day, Marcus left his phone on her nightstand and asked Deja' to grab it. When she picked it up, there was a picture of a baby as the screensaver. Deja' immediately asked, "Whose baby?"

Marcus responded with the name of his oldest son, saying that it was a picture of him when he was a baby.

Inside, Deja' said to herself, *this son is a grown man, why would Marcus have a picture of him as a baby as his screen saver on his phone?* But with no proof she just held it in.

See how warning signs are being presented and she is seeing them all, questioning them all? This relationship was different than any of her previous ones. There was no evidence of cheating, quick rebuttals when questioned, sweetness, kindness, appearance and words of intent for commitment; yet there were still numerous signs of mystery.

This was a merry-go-round. It made you dizzy behind the mask of a good time.

The arguments continued and so did the mysteriousness. Deja' tried to break up with Marcus on at least three occasions. He would return with tears and expressions of love and wanting to be a better man, toting flowers and well-worded cards.

History has a tendency to repeat itself and show up in a different disguise. Deja' would notice that holidays were a common time for them to argue and not be together. Marcus was not always making an escape out of town, but they were not spending holidays together. Instead, they were arguing over text or on the phone. More red flags, but Deja' could not get any proof.

Lesson: Do you need proof, or is your intuition enough?

The mysteriousness—who was this man she was sharing her bed with? Behaviors were not adding up, stories were not adding up, and they sometimes changed when retold at a different time.

Deja' was bugging. Marcus was not as supportive as he could have been when she was going through something that was bothering her. Instead he used it as an opportunity to tear her down and judge her, attempting to cut her down to size.

Marcus would tell Deja' she was a boss whenever she expressed her opinion about something during a conversation, and called her bougee.

Ladies, have you experienced any of this? I share this level of transparency in the hope that if you have, or are living in this reality right now, the red flags are jumping off the page at you.

Going back to the signs God sends: proceed with caution, danger, winding road ahead, unpaved road, sharp turn ahead, etc. What do you do?

The signs were there, woven in with intimacy, no proof of cheating, no disappearing acts, or for lack of a better phrase, none of the obvious signs of betrayal that Deja' was used to seeing.

Then Deja' experienced the death of PaPa, her father in-law, who was like a father to her. When she moved in with Rick at 17, PaPa, his father, was a quiet, kind man who kept to himself but was caring, and when he did speak you listened.

PaPa only let the lion out of the cage when he was really upset about something. But you could watch shows with him and laugh with him, and PaPa never judged you when you made mistakes. PaPa was another father to her.

When he passed, Deja' was hurt. He was the last father figure in her life that was still living, so it was a reminder of every father figure before him who was now gone.

During this time Deja' really needed Marcus to support her. When she found out PaPa was going to pass soon, he did not oppose her going to New York he even encouraged her. He told her to go because she would never forgive herself if she didn't.

The problem comes when a person says to you what is right to say but does not mean it at the core. Marcus tortured Deja' mentally during the drive there, on the trip back, and continued even when she was back at home. Marcus made it all about Rick, practically accusing Deja' of sleeping with Rick, or sneaking and lying about something.

Deja' was transparent with Marcus from the beginning about her past and her current friendship with Rick. When asked a question, Deja' was honest in all her responses.

Yet Marcus tried to minimize her honesty, integrity and character, projecting onto her either how he was currently living, past experiences he'd had with other women in the past perhaps, or simply the way he viewed women as a whole.

Deja' knew for sure now that Marcus did not know her. He continued to batter her during her grief and pain and would not let up, even though she had been 100% honest with him.

This problem passed, but would continue to raise its head periodically. Deja' still pointed out Marcus's behavior, such as an experience at his house with a female neighbor who was supposed to be just a friend. But as women, we know when a woman is throwing you shade about your man. She was definitely throwing shade.

Marcus stood his ground, saying nothing was going on and she was only a friend. Meanwhile, he berated Deja' at every turn about Rick, who was from her past, and lived 700 miles away.

Deja' was completely available to Marcus, she could be reached at any time, and was not traveling to New York for leisure trips every other month. It was only those two trips for the funeral, which happened about seven or eight months into their relationship.

When did Deja' or could Deja' have been messing around? She never hid her phone, nor was it ringing constantly like Marcus's was at all times of day and late in to the night. Yet she was being attacked and accused.

Now here is the grand finale. Rick, with whom she had been like family for many years, sent her and her mom Mia an Amazon Fire stick to plug into her television, allowing them to watch movies that were new in theaters and also had Hulu and Netflix on it, around Deja's birthday. I will truthfully say Deja' did need to take some responsibility for this one. Even after all of Marcus's behavior, she knew to always remain who she was, but Deja' deviated this time.

Marcus would always tell her she revealed too much, and that if she had not shared her past with him, that he would not have felt uncomfortable about Rick. In her mind, she felt that transparency was best. Nonetheless, even you reading this may agree with Marcus or perhaps with Deja's view. That's neutral ground and everyone is entitled to their opinion.

Deja' decided not to tell him right away. She didn't feel she should not have accepted the gift, especially with the way Marcus had been behaving.

Once, after the shade situation, he drove that same neighbor's car to Deja's job and claimed the neighbor wanted him to detail it. Later, he added that she had let him drive it because his car was in the shop—and tried to make it Deja's fault, saying, "You knew my car had to go in the shop, yet you didn't offer help or concern as to how I was going to get around."

Mind games, ladies.

Now, after the shade incident, Marcus said he was going to fall back and put some distance into his friendship with this woman. But a month after that conversation, he was driving her car! Then he told Deja' that the woman said to him, "Why people want to drive your car but don't want to be your man?"

Really!

Marcus claimed she was cut off completely, but a few months later, on Memorial Day morning, who calls him but this woman! When questioned about it, Marcus responded, "She wants me to detail her car."

Deja' said, "Boy, bye!" He was doing too much.

Back to the Fire stick, though. About three weeks after getting the stick, it was bothering her. Deja' and Marcus were having a conversation about him getting a Fire stick and Deja' told him she had one and that it was a gift from Rick.

Initially he said, "I'm not mad, I know you speak and have a friendship with him, but why didn't you tell me sooner?"

Deja' explained that because he would always say she shares too much, she didn't tell him right away, and figured when the topic came up she would share it.

Marcus got another call and had to hang up, but when he called back, he was a different person. Now he was upset and saying confrontational things and it was a complete departure from the previous conversation. It ended in a yelling match where Marcus said, "I will speak to you later," as he often did when they had a disagreement.

The next morning, Marcus sent Deja' a text saying, *I am not dealing with another man being in my life and I am not going to act like I can deal with it so I am going to remove myself from the situation.* He continued, *you withheld information from me for three weeks so as far as I am concerned you are sneaking and lying and there is more going on.*

A week earlier, Marcus had wanted to take yet another trip to New Jersey on a holiday, and expected her to understand. He always had an excuse for his behavior and expected Deja' to understand, but if she did anything at all, he treated it as if it was a felony.

So this argument and breakup happened the week he was supposed to take the trip that she did not agree he should take, and he was trying to convince her that his brother needed him. Perfect time for a breakup, right?

They did not get back together this time, and Marcus did not do his usual, "let's talk" routine, or bring flowers and cards. Instead, when they did text, he took it as an opportunity to tell Deja' how she had hurt him badly and she could now have Rick. Deja was fine with the break up as she had tried to end the relationship several times knowing marcus was not the right fit for her. When he sent the text saying he was removing himself from her life, her response was,"Ok", yet he continued to text with insults.

Marcus continued to push the idea that Deja' was withholding information, and probably sneaking around and talking to Rick on the phone more than she admitted. He took the opportunity to belittle her as much as he could, although he never took responsibility for any of his behavior during their entire relationship. Deja would text back asking him to stop texting her. It was fine, they were done, but he continued because he wanted to try to tear her down and not own any of his bad behavior.

If Deja' dared mention that, Marcus tried to play it down as the past, yet his yesterday still held questionable behavior that was not appropriate and his tomorrow was almost surely predicted to be the same. Meanwhile, Marcus consistently claimed he was working on being a better man. A year was sufficient for Deja' to have given him a chance to become a better man, honestly it was longer than he deserved. Marcus texted once or twice trival things and sent a video chat invite that she ignored. He followed up saying his phone called her by mistake.

Now I mentioned a grand finale a few paragraphs ago, so here it is. Marcus and Deja' spoke back in forth by text a few times, and then stopped speaking completely. A couple of months later, Deja' received some information about a baby registry that had been started in August that had his name listed, along with the name of a woman who lived in New York.

Let me remind you, Marcus and Deja' met in May of that year. When Deja' saw this registry she was shocked! She investigated further and acquired some pictures of the woman and the baby.

The baby was born a year and a half prior to the time Deja' was finding this out—it was born while she and Marcus were together. This woman would have had to be five months pregnant when they met, to add insult to injury.

Marcus and Deja' were barely broken up three months at the time she discovered this baby. Although they had not spoken for about two months, Deja' decided to send him a text with the picture for confirmation. Marcus responded saying, "Wow, I am that important, being investigated months later," instead of just being honest.

Deja' responded, "Wow, only you would respond that way," and went on to say, "You're not that important; I am, because God saw it fit that He expose you to me for who you really are."

Deja' concluded that this discovery was, if for no other reason, closure, reassuring her that the warning signs had been real and she had not been bugging. It was also a sign to let her know to trust herself more, and that she did not always need proof because her gut was enough.

Marcus admitted the child was his, and that he did not know, but as Deja' and he grew in the relationship, he found out but loved her too much and did not want to hurt her.

Ladies, do you see this clearly from the experience of another? I sure hope so. It's the same demon, different package; just this time with mystery and distractions making it hard for Deja' to see clearly, yet presenting the same circumstances.

Marcus was still lying. The baby registry was started three months after he met Deja', therefore he knew from the beginning and apparently was claiming the child, otherwise his name would not have been on the registry with the woman's.

Once again, Deja' had attracted her past. Someone who would use, betray, deceive, and take her for granted.

Do you think that was the baby picture she saw on Marcus's phone? Why were there so many trips for emergencies connected to his brother? The mysteriousness Deja' felt, but could not put her finger on? Why Deja' felt she did not know Marcus?

Meanwhile Marcus, when this secret baby would have been about four months old, was torturing Deja' about going to her father in-law's funeral, accusing her of possibly sneaking around with Rick. Marcus drove home the point that he was not dealing with another man in his life as the reason he decided to remove himself from Deja's life after the fire stick argument.

He claimed to have a problem with her withholding the information about the fire stick for a few weeks before voluntarily, I might add, disclosing it, not by getting busted. That was a betrayal and keeping of a secret? Remember, Marcus used to make statements like, "I trust unless given a reason not to trust" and "As my grandmother used to say, everything comes out in the wash."

Meanwhile, he met Deja' when this woman in New York was five months pregnant. She had the baby when Marcus and Deja' had been dating about five months, and they broke up 11 months later because of the supposed withholding of information about a fire stick.

As you can imagine, Deja' was flabbergasted and in shock. She could not eat for two days. Deja' could accept the breakup over the fire stick situation because she could respect his position about her friendship with Rick although she did not agree with his bias.

She had only known Marcus a short time and never asked him to cut off his ex-wife or female friends yet he expected her to.

Marcus, who had been mysterious and displaying potentially non-committed behavior, had demanded that she cut Rick off. No, she was good with the breakup, because Deja' had only known Marcus for a year and a half. But to think that Marcus wanted her to cut off someone important in her life for him, when he was withholding such an unimaginable secret!

Marcus was indeed unworthy of Deja's love, because he did not have her good interest at heart, let alone her best interests.

Deja' could not eat because she cared for Marcus, had shared her bed with him, and had genuinely had his best interest at heart. Deja' had supported Marcus personally and encouraged him during his struggles, even when she did not agree with all of his choices or his reasoning. She had never shot him down.

Deja' replayed every conversation, every sexual encounter, and every lie that was told. Every suspicion she had all went through her head like a movie as she thought, *Oh my God, this whole thing was a lie from the beginning.* Marcus had targeted her, why she did not know, but she was targeted nonetheless.

Marcus had carried on a year-long relationship with her, all as a game! This was unimaginable to Deja', and an experience she had never had before.

For the men who find themselves flipping through this book, are you seeing the heartache and pain that deception causes? The mental and emotional chaos caused? Are you or have you been Marcus?

Instead of a woman seeing you in your rightful role as a protector, a provider, security and guide, are you seen as an enemy, a thief, confusing and derailing her? When you deceive and damage the heart of the woman you claim to care about, everyone loses, including you.

If you do not see it reading this book, one day you are going to encounter a woman you truly love, and then you will understand because you perhaps, will find yourself paying for the last man's damage. So if you are not ready, avoid women who are looking for commitment and longevity! And once you are ready, be committed to being the man you were created to be!

Note: Women, when he does show up, embrace him, and put him in his rightful place, as king!

The question Deja' asked God was, *I know this was for a purpose; the Devil may never want me to trust again, but I know that is not your agenda Lord, but what is this about? What is the lesson? Why did this happen?*

She knew there was a purpose and a truth for her to know, but what was it? As this book is being written, she still does not have the full answer to that question. Deja' believes part of the lesson was, "you do not need proof", your intuition is enough. She is also confident it aided in her pain-to-change moment. It was part of solidifying the epiphany she recently had from that few weeks of multiple experiences that overwhelmed her and gave her the quickening, leading her to have that one pivotal conversation with her girlfriend, who encouraged her to write this book.

Chapter Thirteen
Embracing Self-Awareness

Deja' believes the enemy came at her aiming a knockout punch, but it was part of a bigger picture for her to share her gift and write this book that has the potential to impact the lives of millions of women. Deja' also believes Marcus was symbolic in a sense, because he came with a lot of distractions, disguising the deception and created a discomfort of sorts that challenged her trust issues.

Prior to this, she had tried hard to strike a balance. This experience caused her to analyze behaviors and patterns with men in her life more clearly, while also coming to the realization that she could feel comfortable not having proof of a betrayal before dismissing someone, and just simply trust her gut.

When you experience multiple betrayals, it can become the window through which you see the world, and cause you to doubt your judgment as being excessively non-trusting, so to create balance you give people too much latitude. Perhaps those events, that happened over the course of a few weeks, and put Deja' into an emotional whirlwind, ushered in a pain that created change.

Marcus's baby being exposed was just a reminder for Deja' to trust herself more and know that these relationship issues were related to her past and it was OK to put pressure on it, just like the challenge she had to walk again after being shot.

Once she let go of the fear of pain and falling, she eventually was able to walk normally. In the same way, the fear and pain brought by men caused her to have a level of fear of heartbreak and uncertainty in every new relationship, and not move too quickly in following her intuition, due to not wanting to apply too much pressure.

This realization has changed her perception of the type of men she is used to picking, and strengthened her ability to trust herself in this area despite her past. She has excelled in every other area of her life, but the relationship challenge is still evolving.

Today, she feels she has reached a new freedom in this area. This overall quickening from the multiple events of those few weeks brought about a change in Deja' as a person and as a woman. She needed to set boundaries in her life regarding her heart and interactions with people around her and in her life as a whole.

Not all has been made clear to her yet, but Deja' is resolute that it will be. But for now, she can proclaim she remembers clearly the day of the pivot. It was at the height of her pain, during those weeks of feeling overwhelmed about four events that included some issues at work, love relationship, family and friend issues that hurt her and brought about the comment to Mia, "I am all things to all people but I am nothing to anyone."

And then the pivot came. Deja' was now in a different headspace about life and people. She was a blank canvas, and believes that is how her friend was able to break through and bring her to a place of agreeing to write this book.

Deja' believes in her heart that it can be a platform for her passion to help women overcome the hand they were dealt, by hearing her story and walking with her through her jouney. Although Deja's life is not perfect nor does she profess to have overcome all, and therefore a qualified expert, she however does know, that some of what she went through could derail, destroy and potentially cause someone to lose who they are. Her jouney serves as an example that your issues can be overcome. Her passion is to aide and encourage others to stand and fight even if your life is a mess. Some pains are self inflicted by poor choices and not having boundaries. As women we tend to give too much room for people to hurt us. Our instincts and intuition need to be a stronger guide. Many times there are obvious dysfunctions, but we often wait until it is causing us pain to move out of it. Preventing it from causing us pain by lowering our tolerance level for dysfunction is mandatory and part of self love.

Deja' is looking forward to continuing her journey in life, chasing her dreams, living in peace and joy, and never letting anyone steal that from her. Deja' is also embarking on something new, in that she did not have writing a book in her grand plan, so God is moving and she is excited to see where He is taking her.

Deja' plans to continue in real estate, which she is also passionate about. She is still striving toward early retirement and freedom from a job. She is committed to continuing to be a good leader, a loving friend, sister, niece, and daughter to Mia.

Deja' loves her mom, forgives her for her shortcomings due to her own childhood abuses, and is extremely proud of her. Deja' watched her mom endure many struggles and make the choice to live and not die.

Mia is a woman who chose to fight for her life and trusted God, when she was at her lowest point, to give her another chance at life so she could do better. Well, God did and she did too!

Mia went back to school, got her driver's license, and started working in the nursing field, where she has been for about 15 years now. Mia is in her sixties, but looks like she is in her forties, and bears no scars from the indescribable life she lived. You would be hard pressed to look at Mia and imagine the pain and trials she endured.

Deja' is grateful to God for saving Mia's life and allowing Mia to be in her life. It gives her great joy to see Mia whole, and be able to love Mia and herself.

They talk every day and Deja' visits Mia often. They take trips together, laugh and can talk about anything. Mia is her mom and her friend. Deja' cannot imagine her life without Mia.

The dream and passion to help other women overcome is also something Deja' is excited about and looking forward to. Deja' wants to help young women learn how to see and feel the signs God throws up as well as impart to them the necessity of having a source that is greater than yourself and anyone you know.

Deja' wants to help women practice and implement a process in their lives that keeps them in a place of peace and wholeness. Deja' desires to impart what her own processes are, and share the rest of her journey with other women as an example of overcoming, because it is indeed a lifetime journey.

She has laid herself bare in this book—the good and bad of her, as well as the strong and weak moments of her life, without shame. There is so much more that was not included in this book that Deja' believes is better conveyed in a live setting and plans to share it with many women during her encounters with them, as they are personal, intimate and are worth sharing as part of helping other women with their process and journey in life.

If Deja' is able to help one woman fight and not give up; help one woman embrace her mistakes and learn from them; help one woman forgive herself or her mother and learn to love herself and realize her worth, it will be more than worth any part of her that the enemy attempted to destroy by bringing pain, betrayal, or confusion, and Deja' would willingly take the journey again if it was all for the purpose of getting her to her destiny and unveiling a gift that can help millions of women overcome.

So I pray that each person reading this book has received something from it, and that it has had a positive impact on your life. I hope it has given you some tools to put in your kit bag that you will be able to use along your life's journey. Wisdom is learning from someone else's mistakes.

I pray that it has helped you heal some broken places, and given you a deeper awareness of yourself. That it inspired you to forgive yourself and people who have hurt you. That you walk away knowing that you are not alone in this life of ups and downs, and that as women our stories share many similarities.

We bruise deep, love hard, and soar high when given the opportunity. We are all worthy of love, respect, and to be cherished.

It starts with knowing that God loves you—therefore, loving yourself is not a choice but a mandate. Loving yourself is a prerequisite of wholeness, healthy thinking, and self-esteem. You need each of those traits to be successful in life. They give you strength, determination, and the ability to follow through and not give up, as well as the ability to identify when something is trying to destroy you, and the courage to get out, while also helping you to look in the mirror and feel beautiful, special and irreplaceable.

Commit to love yourself, and I look forward to seeing you out in the world and you sharing your story of overcoming with me someday. Be blessed.

Note: please listen to the songs listed in the introduction of this book and read the next few pages, which contain testimonies from people who wanted to share how Deja's life and story impacted and helped to change them and theirs.

About the Author

Kisha Taylor was born in Brooklyn, NY. At a young age, she had to learn how to navigate the real world of hard knocks. She received a formal education from Binghamton University and Baruch College, where she studied accounting and psychology. She however learned most of the life lessons she shares with others from her own experiences and those she witnessed in other peoples lives. Kisha has done lots of healing work on herself along with research over the years to become knowledgeable in "why people act the way they do". She started with herself as the first client as someone who struggled with abandonment issues most of her young adult life. Involuntarily, she became council to many, simply by sharing principles on how to survive abuse, overcome life's challenges, and healthy ways of handling personal mistakes along ones journey while not surrendering to self-defeat. By her influence, personal example and encouragement, Kisha has made a positive impact in peoples lives who lost hope and struggled with self-esteem and depression. She instead deposited hope, strength, and inspiration in order to aide others in healing, self-love, forgiveness and the confidence to overcome.

Acknowledge
The Impact

I met Deja' when she was 21 years old. My impression was that she was wiser than her years, very mature, loyal, and had her head on straight. I immediately took a liking to her. There was something about her inner self, her inner spirit, that attracted me to her and from that day to this one she's been my sista and I'd do anything for her. I trust her with my life. We once had a conversation in which I told her that I trusted her enough to make medical and financial decisions for me if I was unable, because I think her judgment is as sound as mine. Now how many people can you honestly say that about? I can't count three! Well, that's my heartfelt summation about my friend, my sista Deja'.

Monica

When I first met Deja', I did not know what I was in for. I always felt that I was not perfect, but I was meant to work toward perfection. This I got from my mom, Rita, and my dad, Charles, who were Jehovah's Witnesses. I misunderstood Deja' being familiar with and having a understanding as to what a religious person was and a God-fearing person is. After all had been said and done, I came to the conclusion that she and I are God-fearing people. As New York City corrections officers, I really believe we had to set examples, and in so doing, we had to strive to be the best at meeting our responsibilities. Deja' and I have known each other close to 20 years or more. We would be back and forth about security attentiveness and mostly we both enjoyed and respected the conversations about God. After eight or nine years of service together, I began to truly understand Deja' and what she was working toward: a closer relationship with God. She felt the environment in which we worked impeded her personal progress, which you have to respect, but I did not agree with her leaving the job. What I took from her was the strength she had in a lot of areas of life: God first, and relationships. Don't play with them was her philosophy, be true to your friends, and when selecting friends, it's quality not quantity that matters. With God's grace, Deja' has been and continues to be blessed. She always looks for the beauty inside of a person and she does not give up easily on people. She loves you even when you are not lovable. She loves herself, but is always leaving room for improvement. She knows she is not perfect, but thanks God for unconditionally loving her even though she has been through various storms. She put her trust in God and in turn she continues to shine. She is and always will be my homegirl and true friend. I will love her until death do us part.

Jordan

I have had the pleasure of being a part of Deja's life for over two decades. She is very communicative, honest, inspirational, loving, self-sacrificing, and solution-oriented, and is a person of action. The aforementioned are just a few areas in which I strive to emulate her. Looking back over the years, I can honestly say I'm a totally different person because she came into my life. I could write a book detailing all the examples of how she impacted my life, but I will just write about the most recent example. Deja' is a very successful real estate investor. She started her business a few years ago. I was excited for her. I watched from the sidelines as she read books and attended seminars to learn all she could about the business. I knew she would be successful because as I wrote, she is solution-oriented and a person of action. Her rapid success inspired a childhood girlfriend to follow in her footsteps. I had always wanted to start a real-estate business. Deja' has seen old goal sheets of mine dated as far back as 1988, stating my desire to get rich in the real-estate business. I didn't start my business until May 2014. This was after Deja' had built a successful real-estate business. Her success inspired me to take action after not doing so for over 26 years. To sum up how I feel about her impact on my life, I often say to her, "I am me because of you."

Malcolm
TDAD Realty Co.

I have been blessed to have Deja' as part of my journey in this life, and am grateful to god that our paths have crossed and we have remained friends throughout the years. I came to love Deja' over the years because she has repeatedly demonstrated that she is loyal. Loyalty and fidelity are very rare qualities in the world today, but they are still highly desirable traits that we seek in our family members, loved ones and friends. Her continual devotion and faithfulness are not blind but they are constant. Her allegiance is coupled with honesty and integrity. Deja' will stand by you but she will also speak her truth in any situation. Deja' is supportive of her family and friends and dedicated to her loved ones. It takes an emotionally strong and resilient person to make herself available to render assistance to those in her sphere when called upon and to make time to give of herself regardless of all the obligations that she has already committed to. Deja' is a priceless treasure. I love Deja' and I am fortunate to have her in my life. She is a blessed soul and I believe that the god of Abraham has called her to make her mark on this world in the manner that he will determine and in the time frame that he has already laid out. This book is a vessel and I pray that its inspired words will create ripples and waves in your life that can generate the tides that will spark positive tides of change in your lives.

Lisa

Deja' is the epitome of a leader. I have known her for over a decade and she has taught me so much throughout the years. The way she can take control of any situation and not lose her cool is amazing. I've watched her handle so many different situations and people and all in a peaceful manner. I have taken that and applied it to my life. Anytime I am faced with an obstacle that needs me to think outside the box I think of Deja' and how she would handle it. She is always there to talk to and give advice. I remember this one time a few years ago...I had to make a tough decision of either staying in my current role or moving on to something different. I texted her right away and I took her advice and now I couldn't be happier. I am now a proud homeowner because of that advice. As a woman it can be difficult in the career world but watching women like Deja' motivates you to do better and be better.

Subrena

In 1986 I had a life-changing event. See, I became a mother. I asked my then-best friend to be my daughter's godmother. She was just a teenager herself, but without hesitation she said yes. I'm not sure if she knew what she was getting into, because I was not so sure myself. We were teenage girls from the hood but we made a promise, a commitment to each other and to this precious little girl. Yeah, Deja' was my homie, my ride or die, but being a godmother was a big responsibility. Even back then she took the bull by the horns. She was not one of those "godmother in name only" people who would send you a gift for your birthday and Christmas. See, my children were fortunate enough to have her every day of their lives. Two more babies, two more godchildren she took on. She never missed a beat. The hugs and kisses, the spankings, motivational talks, direction and guidance, and yes, those gifts. That first little girl is almost 31 years old and Deja' and I are still best friends. She is as present and active in their lives today as the day she first said yes. Our lives have changed greatly. We made it out of the hood and are upper middle class even. We often reminisce over those driving factors that made it all happen. No one could have ever asked for a better godmother for her children. How incredibly blessed we are to have her in our lives. And as we end every conversation, I will say now again—love you girl!

Tyra

Deja' is a brilliant and a unique person. She's gracious, honest, loyal, giving and has a tremendous heart which allows her to forgive and forget. Deja' is unendingly determined and disciplined. She is no-nonsense, fair, but a firm leader with integrity who believes that consistency and hard work pays off. I am so often inspired by her actions that at times when I am faced with a decision I will ask myself, what would Deja' do in this situation?

Rick

Not everyone in life is blessed to meet such a spiritual, loving and caring individual who puts others before herself. I am one of the lucky ones who have had the privilege to have her in my life. Deja's wisdom and grace are unique. She is a light in my life. Her ability to calm a person down and ease their worries is unlike anything I've ever seen before. I call her my counselor and my spiritual guide. Thank you for all you've done. Not just for me but for all the other people whose lives you have touched so deeply and for those who you will continue to touch. Friends like you are a rare gift. Love you always.

Ana

What I admire about my best friend Deja' is she is so outgoing. She gives you comfort, hopes of prosperity and laughter. I've known Deja' since the fourth grade and growing up, I watched her achieve her goals. I can't help but be so proud of her. Deja' has inspired me to believe in myself, and to believe that I can do anything I put my mind to. The one thing I admire most about Deja' is she loves her family, even though she's had some rough times with them. She knows family is important to have in your life. Deja' is the type to encourage you when you don't believe in yourself. She gives you encouraging and spiritual words to lift you up. She's a believer!

Tracy

I was raised to believe that people come into your life for a reason and when they do you should try to understand their purpose in your life. When I met Deja' ten years ago I had a lot of different things going on. She was very open and shared a piece of her story with me which gave me the hope that this too shall pass. It was very encouraging to see a young woman go through a similar situation and watch how she has been able to press past it and accomplish so much. My prayer is that through her bravery in sharing her story, other young women and men will allow the words in this book to encourage them as well as press on towards their goals in life.

Kawanna

Double dutch, making up plays, fistfights, sharing clothes, dressing up like twins, pricking our fingers to become "blood sisters," listening to "Rapper's Delight," getting our hind parts whooped, hanging out in Bed-Stuy some weekends and New Jersey others, sharing feelings about boy crushes—we did it all! Literally my God-given sister! Deja' has always been the level-headed one, very analytical and wise beyond her years. If anyone has determination and grit, it's Deja'. Precision and accuracy have always been her strong suits. She imparts knowledge into my life and challenges my thought process. Her spirituality and resilience are beyond measure. Deja's success is no surprise to me. It was inevitable. I love my sister and she will always be my she-ro. Deja', I am proud of you!

Dawn

CPSIA information can be obtained
at www.ICGtesting.com
Printed in the USA
FFOW02n1548130418
46256112-47671FF